STAHR

A Romance

by

F. SCOTT FITZGERALD

The only surviving title page for the novel.—F. Scott Fitzgerald Papers,
Princeton University Library

"The Last of the Novelists"

F. Scott Fitzgerald and

THE LAST TYCOON

By Matthew J. Bruccoli

JEFFERIES PROFESSOR OF ENGLISH

University of South Carolina

SOUTHERN ILLINOIS UNIVERSITY PRESS

Carbondale and Edwardsville

FEFFER & SIMONS, INC.

London and Amsterdam

Previously unpublished material from manuscripts and
notes for The Last Tycoon is published with the generous
permission of Frances Scott Fitzgerald Smith and
Harold Ober Associates. All rights remain the property
of the Estate of F. Scott Fitzgerald.

Excerpts from The Last Tycoon by F. Scott Fitzgerald,
Copyright 1941 Charles Scribner's Sons, renewal
Copyright © 1969 Frances Scott Fitzgerald Smith, are
reprinted by permission of Charles Scribner's Sons and
The Bodley Head (The Bodley Head Scott Fitzgerald
Vol. 1).

Library of Congress Cataloging in Publication Data

Bruccoli, Matthew Joseph, 1931–
"The last of the novelists"

Includes bibliographical references.
    1. Fitzgerald, Francis Scott Key, 1896–1940.
The last tycoon. I. Title.
PS3511.I9L354   813'.5'2   77-4381
ISBN 0-8093-0820-7

In Memory of

Mary Gervasi Bruccoli

"I am the last of the novelists for a long time now."

"I look out at it — and I think it is the most beautiful

history in the world. It is the history of me and

of my people. And if I came here yesterday like

Sheilah I should still think so. It is the

history of all aspiration — not just the American

dream but the human dream and if I came at the end

of it that too is a place in the line of the pioneers."

F. Scott Fitzgerald, Notes for The Last Tycoon

Contents

"*The Last of the Novelists*"

F. Scott Fitzgerald and

THE LAST TYCOON

Chronology / 1939-1940

January 1939   Termination of Fitzgerald's MGM contract (July 1937–Jan. 1939)

February 1939   Fitzgerald works on *Winter Carnival* with Budd Schulberg for United Artists

March 1939   Fitzgerald works on *Air Raid* for Paramount

May 1939   Fitzgerald begins blocking out novel

18 July 1939   Fitzgerald offers Kenneth Littauer of *Collier's* serial rights to novel

August 1939   Fitzgerald works on *Open that Door* for Universal

September 1939   Fitzgerald works on *Everything Happens at Night* for 20th Century-Fox and *Raffles* for Goldwyn

29 September 1939   Fitzgerald sends plan for novel to Littauer

November 1939   Fitzgerald sends first section to Littauer; Littauer declines to make advance

28 November 1939   Fitzgerald breaks off negotiations with *Collier's* and offers serial to *The Saturday Evening Post*

January 1940   Publication of "Pat Hobby's Christmas Wish," first of 17 Pat Hobby stories in *Esquire*

March-Summer 1940   Fitzgerald works on "Babylon Revisited" for Lester Cowan

November 1940   First heart attack

21 December 1940   Death of F. Scott Fitzgerald

1 /

Preliminaries

CLOSE EXAMINATION OF THE MANUSCRIPTS AND NOTES FOR THE unfinished novel known as *The Last Tycoon* allows us to gauge the state of F. Scott Fitzgerald's work-in-progress at the time of his death and thereby to re-assess this work properly. It is evident that in the case of work-in-progress authorial intention is the crucial consideration for interpretation and evaluation. In such a work we must scrutinize the evidence for clues to its evolution; and it is obligatory that we determine how far the work had really progressed.

All critical judgment of *The Last Tycoon* has been strongly influenced by Edmund Wilson's redaction of the material. His text—still the only published text—is misleading because it presents Fitzgerald's working drafts in a finished form. In addition to emending Fitzgerald, Wilson formed chapters out of episodes; but the reader of the Wilson text has no way of knowing how much editorial improvement he is absorbing.

Examination of Fitzgerald's drafts reveals that he regarded none of this material as finished. There are no final drafts—only latest working drafts. After Chapter One there are no chapters, and even this chapter is marked for rewrite. Indeed, it is by no means certain that Fitzgerald knew how he would end his novel. *The Last Tycoon* is not really an "unfinished novel," if that term describes a work that is partly finished. The only way to regard it is as material toward a novel.

Speculation about the unwritten portion of the novel soon becomes futile. Although this problem is extremely interesting, we cannot speak with confidence about it. Fitzgerald's undated last outline provides only topics or ideas for the thirteen unwritten episodes. The most useful approach to the study of the novel is in terms of what Fitzgerald accomplished—not of what he was planning. His novel had developed in ways that were significantly different from his other work. Most notably, Monroe Stahr is a hero without a flaw. Unlike Amory Blaine, Anthony Patch, Jay Gatsby, or Dick Diver who are afflicted with character weaknesses, Monroe Stahr is intact up to episode 17, the last episode Fitzgerald wrote. It is clear that he was to be defeated in the end, but Fitzgerald plants no seeds of self-destruction in Stahr's character. Although Stahr's defeat is connected with his love for Kathleen, she is not the cause. Stahr's affair with Kathleen only provides Brady with a weapon to use against him.

Fitzgerald was a life-long hero-worshipper, but he was not able to create an unflawed hero until he himself was in his forties. It is meaningful that Monroe Stahr is the first hero in a Fitzgerald novel with a successful career: Amory and Anthony have no occupations; Gatsby's business activities are shadowy; and Dick Diver abandons his promising career. But Stahr is totally committed to his work and the responsibility that goes with it. He is Fitzgerald's only complete professional. Moreover, Stahr is immune to the emotional bankruptcy that is epidemic in Fitzgerald's work after 1930. A lonely young widower with a pervasive sense of loss, he is nonetheless not broken by loss, and he retains the capacity to love again. Stahr's one terrible mistake comes when he delays the decision to go away with Kathleen by one day—and during that day he loses her. If one is compelled to seek a flaw in Stahr, it is that he has an excess of reason or discipline; but it would be difficult to support this reading.

Apart from the narrative problems with Cecelia, the most serious problem in the drafts is that Stahr's attraction to Kathleen is not entirely convincing. Stahr is no dreamy Jay Gatsby stunned by a rich girl. He has his pick of glamorous women, none of whom interests him. Then Stahr falls in love at first sight with Kathleen. Something more than her resemblance to his dead wife is required. Kathleen is beautiful, but Stahr is inundated by beauty. Sex doesn't account for it either, even though he has presumably gone for a long time without a woman. Again, Stahr would have no trouble finding someone beautiful to sleep with. Raymond Chandler observed that Stahr was "magnificent when he sticks to the business of dealing with pictures and the people he has to use to make them; the instant his personal life as a love-hungry and exhausted man enters the picture, he becomes just another guy with too much money and nowhere to go." [1]

One of the standard lines of Fitzgerald criticism is that his women are tougher than his men; that in what almost amounts to a reversal of traditional sexual roles, the men tend to be romantically weak, whereas the women are strong. In *The Last Tycoon* Fitzgerald created his only strong novel hero. As a consequence, perhaps, the characterization of Kathleen is not compelling. Stahr so dominates the reader's attention and imagination that no one else in the novel can compete with him. It is possible that at forty-four Fitzgerald no longer felt as keenly about women as he once had. That Fitzgerald sensed a deficiency in his treatment of Kathleen is revealed by his note: "Where will the warmth come from in this. Why does he think she's warm. Warmer than the voice in Farewell. My girls were all so warm and full of promise. The sea at night. What can I do to make it honest and different?"

A clue to Fitzgerald's difficulties with Kathleen is provided by one of his working titles, "The Love of the Last Tycoon." The novel has a split focus. It is a love story and a character study of an American archetype. Stahr dominates the novel, and the strongest scenes are those that show him at work. There are many ironies in Fitzgerald's career, but none is more eloquent than that the "laureate of the Jazz Age" became the admiring creator of a worker-boss. Nevertheless, this irony is not surprising in view of Fitzgerald's life-long respect for achievement and his guilt about his own irresponsibility.

The Last Tycoon has always been read as a Hollywood novel—a novel about the movies. Attention to the setting has obscured an aspect of the novel that is at least of equal significance: Monroe Stahr as businessman-hero. It is a commonplace observation that America, the great business nation, has produced few major business novels. The businessmen of our literature are largely unsatisfactory because they are seen from the outside by authors who are not sure what their characters really do. Howells' Silas Lapham, James' Christopher Newman, and Lewis' George F. Babbitt are travesties. Curtis Jadwin is shown at work in Norris' *The Pit*, but he is not a convincing character. It is noteworthy that Lapham, Newman, and Jadwin reject their business careers. Little space is devoted to Alfred Eaton's business activities in O'Hara's *From the Terrace*. The only searching studies of the American as businessman are Dreiser's Frank Cowperwood, Cozzens' Henry Worthington, and Monroe Stahr.

Although it is far from certain that *The Last Tycoon* was Fitzgerald's final title, it is clear that Fitzgerald conceived Stahr as a "tycoon." The tentative title "The Love of The Last Tycoon: A Western" is instructive, for the subtitle connects Stahr with all the other poor boys who went West to seek their fortunes. Stahr is also in the tradition of the Horatio Alger heroes: from office boy to boss.

The interest in the American Dream is not a late development in Fitzgerald's work. He was fascinated by success—both personally and as a theme—throughout his career. Ambitious poor boys abound in his work. Fitzgerald believed devoutly in success, but not with a simple-minded acceptance. He understood that achievement rarely matches aspiration. After all, he had lived his own bitter drama of success: The author of *This Side of Paradise* at twenty-four; the author of *The Great Gatsby* at twenty-nine; a crack-up case at thirty-nine. All through his childhood he was aware of his father's business failure and his maternal grandfather's success, and was sensitive to his situation as a poor boy at rich-boy schools. Fitzgerald's response was not the seething resentment of a revolutionary, but rather envy qualified by the recognition of the limitations of success. Ambition was not a pejorative term for Fitzgerald. In his way he was as ambitious as any Ragged Dick or Monroe Stahr.

The interpretation of *The Last Tycoon* as a respectful study of the American business hero is enforced by a note Fitzgerald made for a projected scene in which Stahr is told to quit work by his doctors.

The idea fills Stahr with a horror that I must write a big scene to bring off. Such a scene as has never been written. The scene that to

Stahr is the equivalent to that of an amorous man being told that he is about to be castrated. In other words, the words of the doctor fill Stahr with a horror that I must be able to convey to the laziest reader—the blow to Stahr and the utter unwillingness to admit that at this point, 35 years old, his body should refuse to serve him and carry on these plans which he has built up like a pyramid of fairy sky-scrapers in his imagination.

He has survived the talkies, the depression, carried his company over terrific obstacles and done it all with a growing sense of king-liness—of some essential difference which he could not help feeling between himself and the ordinary run of man and now from the mere accident of one organ of his body refusing to pull its weight, he is in-capacitated from continuing. Let him go through every stage of re-volt.

Such a scene as has never been written. It is not forcing the evidence to claim that this phrase indicates Fitzgerald's sense of identifica-tion with Stahr. Like his hero, Fitzgerald was working against fail-ing health. With the irony by which life sometimes improves on lit-erature, Fitzgerald died of a heart attack while writing about his dying hero.

Stahr possesses an impressive mastery of movie-making, but he does not actually make them. He functions as a leader and super-vises the people who make the movies. Stahr does not write screen-plays or direct movies or edit film; but he tells all of these people how to do their jobs better. It diminishes Stahr to classify him as an administrator, or even as a producer. Stahr is, as he claims, "The unity"—like a novelist.

As a boy Stahr wanted to be the person who had all the keys and knew where everything was. In running the studio he delegates very little—both because he does not have much confidence in his sub-ordinates and because everyone has learned to depend on Stahr. His work is his life; and he would rather be dead than deprived of work. In every possible way Stahr is a refutation of all the clichés about movie executives. Endowed with supreme intelligence and taste, he has elevated an art form without being an artist. There is no criti-cism of Stahr in the pages Fitzgerald wrote. Even in the scene with the union organizor, Stahr behaves foolishly but understandably and sympathetically. Bitterly unhappy and pathetically drunk, the frail, sick leader tries to beat up Brimmer himself.

One of the remarkable aspects of the novel is the extent to which Fitzgerald was able to project himself into Stahr and understand his allegiances, although Fitzgerald did not share them. Fitzgerald—while not politically active—had liberal convictions, but Stahr is a conservative. A self-made man, Stahr believes that anyone with ability can succeed, and resists any attempt by outsiders to interfere with his studio, his people. Even though Stahr admits to having originated the treatment of screenwriters that Fitzgerald bitterly resented, Stahr's policies are justified in terms of his responsibilities. When Stahr says that writers are "unstable" and that "they are not equipped for authority," Brimmer does not contradict him. Fitzgerald may have smiled ruefully when he wrote these words, but he did not violate the integrity of the characterization. From Stahr's position writers are undependable, and he will not yield power to them. For many authors the writing of fiction is an opportunity to live another life. In writing *The Last Tycoon* Fitzgerald granted himself the chance to run a studio, and found that he would have run it much the way Stahr did.

It is an overstatement to claim that *The Last Tycoon* was developing as a political fable, but it is impossible to ignore what might be called the presidential theme in the novel as Fitzgerald associates Stahr with American leaders. Presidential references echo throughout the novel. Stahr's first name is Monroe. In Chapter One, Cecelia, Wylie White, and Schwartze visit Andrew Jackson's home. Prince Agge and Boxley see Stahr as a Lincolnesque figure, and Boxley's recognition is specific: "he had been reading Lord Charnwood and he recognized that Stahr like Lincoln was a leader carrying on a long war on many fronts; almost single-handed he had moved pictures sharply forward through a decade, to a point where the content of the 'A productions' was wider and richer than that of the stage. Stahr was an artist only, as Mr. Lincoln was a general, perforce and as a layman." [2] And there is even the comic scene involving the telephone talk with the orang-outang who looks like President McKinley; at first Stahr thinks the call is from President Roosevelt. In the unwritten part of the novel Fitzgerald planned to have Stahr wander around Washington, D.C., sick. By means of these presidential associations Fitzgerald tried to place Stahr in the tradition of the American leaders, to endow him with a largeness of character that goes beyond the movie industry. The Lincoln connection is not far-fetched: Stahr is another poor boy who rose to a position of enormous responsibility without losing his humane qualities. From log cabin to the White House; from the Bronx to Hollywood. Stahr is the last tycoon, the last of the paternalistic bosses who takes full responsibility for his business. He is a production man, not a money man; and he is an anachronism, under attack from both the capitalists and the communists. He represents an older American tradition of personal responsibility, which is being defeated by the forces of collectivism. Unlike Thalberg, who fought for a bigger share of the profits, Stahr is not interested in money. He is literally working himself to death because he needs to exercise responsibility, and because there is nothing else he would rather do. But the financiers and the lawyers are taking over the studio. The novel marks the end of a phase of American capitalism—the end of individual responsibility in industry.

Robert Sklar has written that Fitzgerald was the last major American novelist "to grow up believing in the genteel romantic ideals that pervaded late nineteenth-century American culture," and argues that "overcoming the genteel tradition was also, in Fitzgerald's case, the prerequisite for creating lasting art." [3] The second part of Sklar's thesis can be challenged, for it is by no means clear that Fitzgerald rejected the standards of his boyhood. Monroe Stahr is a 1935 incarnation of the nineteenth-century American hero—the self-made man who embodies the principles of integrity and responsibility. Perhaps, then, the mutual allegiances of Stahr and Fitzgerald provide the key to the meaning of the moving note, "I am the last of the novelists for a long time now." That comment does not refer to technique or to form. It can only be understood in terms of theme and, above all, character. Fitzgerald believed in ordered social structures and in the role of individual character in maintaining them. His concept of character was romanticized, however, for he also believed in great men. Stahr represents the twenty-year development of the aristocratic romantic egotism introduced in Amory Blaine. For all of Amory's inchoate rebelliousness and iconoclasm, he is in quest of values that will satisfy his need to shape society while at the same time fulfilling his uniqueness. This attitude is a form of *noblesse oblige*—with the character's sense of duty stemming from a conviction of his special ability. It can be differentiated from that of the Hemingway hero who generates a private set of rules in the absence of any belief in social order. The Hemingway code is built on controlled despair. Fitzgerald was a believer. He grew up believing in the promises of America. He believed in the possibilities of life. He believed in character. He believed in decency, honor, courage, responsibility. More than any other Fitzgerald hero, Monroe Stahr exemplifies these qualities. That may be why F. Scott Fitzgerald thought of him as "the last tycoon"—and of himself as the "last of the novelists."

2 /

Backgrounds

THE REMOTE INCEPTION OF *The Last Tycoon* CAN BE ATTRIBUTED to 14 September 1936, the date of Hollywood producer Irving Thalberg's death. Five days later F. Scott Fitzgerald wrote to C. O. Kalman: "Talbert's final collapse is the death of an enemy for me, though I liked the guy enormously. He had an idea that his wife and I were playing around, which was absolute nonsense, but I think even so that he killed the idea of either Hopkins or Frederick Marsh doing 'Tender is the Night.' " [1] Samuel Marx, who was then MGM story editor, recalls that Fitzgerald woke Thalberg with a late-night alcoholic phone call in 1934 to try to sell him *Tender*. [2]

On 16 October 1936 Fitzgerald informed Maxwell Perkins, his Scribners editor: "I have a novel planned, or rather I should say conceived, which fits much better into the circumstances, but neither by this inheritance nor in view of the general financial situation do I see clear to undertake it. It is a novel certainly as long as Tender Is The Night, and knowing my habit of endless corrections and revisions, you will understand that I figure it at two years." [3] Nothing further was forthcoming about this project. There is no evidence that Fitzgerald was thinking about Irving Thalberg as the subject for the novel; but the chronological connection is intriguing, since he wrote this letter less than two months after Thalberg's death.

Although he did not know Thalberg well, the producer was precisely the kind of man who could capture Fitzgerald's imagination because Thalberg represented the qualities that Fitzgerald admired.

The most brilliant of the Hollywood producers, Irving Thalberg had taste, intelligence, and personal style. Already the leading Hollywood producer in his twenties, Thalberg—more than anyone else of his time—raised the quality of the movies. He was, in the language of *This Side of Paradise*, a personage.

Irving Grant Thalberg—the "boy wonder" of Hollywood—was born in Brooklyn on 30 May 1899, the son of William and Henrietta Heyman Thalberg. His parents were of German-Alsatian Jewish stock. William was a lace importer, and the family enjoyed a middle-class standard of living. Thalberg was not a poor boy, unlike Monroe Stahr. Henrietta was fiercely ambitious for her son, who had been born a blue baby and was not expected to have a long life.

Thalberg attended Brooklyn Boys' High School until 1916, when he came down with rheumatic fever. After recovering, he studied in night school and went to work as a secretary-stenographer. In 1918 he was employed by Carl Laemmle at the Universal Pictures office in New York. Laemmle took Thalberg to California on an inspection trip and left him at the studio. When Laemmle returned, he made Thalberg the studio manager at twenty.

Dissatisfied with his salary at Universal, Thalberg joined Louis B. Mayer as Vice-President of the Mayer Company in 1923. When Metro-Goldwyn-Mayer was formed by Loew's in 1924, Thalberg became Second Vice-President and Supervisor of Production. Thalberg, Louis B. Mayer, and J. Robert Rubin—"the Mayer Group"—participated in the profits of MGM. Thalberg's capacity for work became a Hollywood legend, along with his taste and perfectionism. He routinely insisted on expensive retakes to improve films that were considered completed. His films at MGM included *The Merry Widow* (1925), *The Big Parade* (1925), *Ben-Hur* (1926), *The Broadway Melody* (1929), *The Big House* (1930), *Anna Christie* (1930), *Trader Horn* (1931), *The Sin of Madelon Claudet* (1931), *Grand Hotel* (1932), and *Rasputin and the Empress* (1932).

Thalberg was a small man—5 feet 6 inches and about 120 pounds. He spoke quietly and had good manners, but could be tough. In 1927 Thalberg married actress Norma Shearer, and the marriage was regarded as a great success. They had two children. The Thalbergs lived quietly, for his health was always precarious.

Bad feeling between the Mayer Group and Loew's developed in 1929 when Nicholas Schenck, president of Loew's, tried to sell Loew's and MGM to William Fox. Mayer and Thalberg opposed the deal, which was stymied by the stock-market crash and the threat of anti-trust proceedings. Loew's placated the Mayer Group with a large cash bonus, but Thalberg was not satisfied. He felt that his share of the profits was incommensurate with his responsibility for the success of MGM. In 1929 the division of the profits was: Mayer, 53 percent; Thalberg, 20 percent, Rubin, 27 percent. A new contract was negotiated that raised Thalberg's share to 30 percent by lowering Mayer's to 43 percent. Mayer resented his young partner's financial ambitions, but Thalberg continued to press for a larger share; by 1932 Mayer and Thalberg each received 37½ percent of the profits. In 1932 Thalberg announced that he wanted to quit MGM. Schenck persuaded him to stay by offering a stock option. During these negotiations Thalberg and Mayer became estranged as Mayer, a powerful ego, felt that he was being disparaged by an ungrateful protégé. That same year Thalberg collapsed from overwork. While he was recovering Mayer and Schenck hired David O. Selznick as a producer at MGM without consulting Thalberg, and he felt that he had been betrayed. In 1933 when Thalberg was en route to Europe MGM instituted a 50 percent pay cut, which Thalberg opposed because the studio was making money. While Thalberg was vacationing in Europe he received a cable from Mayer informing him that he had been removed as MGM production head. Although Mayer insisted that the move was designed to protect Thalberg's health by relieving him of pressure, Thalberg was angered and hurt. When he returned he was given his own production unit. There was no change in his salary or percentage.

Thalberg's reaction to the Screen Writers Guild is not clear. His biographer, Bob Thomas, states that Thalberg opposed the Guild and that he joined with Darryl F. Zanuck of Twentieth Century-Fox to support the Screen Playwrights. According to Thomas, Thalberg defeated a strike vote by the Guild by promising to shut MGM: "For if you proceed with this strike, *I shall close down the entire plant*, without a single exception." [4] However, Samuel Marx, who was then MGM story editor, insists, "Thalberg had nothing to do with the forming of the Screen Playwrights, either—he was in

Europe through the spring of 1933, when it began. . . . In a very short time he assumed a neutral position." [5]

Thalberg came to feel that Mayer was lowering the standards of MGM films and that he was failing to cooperate fully with the Thalberg unit. Their estrangement became increasingly bitter. A new source of antagonism was provided in 1935 when Thalberg began planning the I. G. Thalberg Corporation, which would distribute through Loew's but be independent of MGM. Mayer opposed the plan, and a compromise was worked out that would enable Thalberg to form his new company in 1939. Irving Thalberg died of pneumonia in September 1936.

The outstanding films made at MGM by Thalberg's unit were *The Barretts of Wimpole Street* (1934), *China Seas* (1935), *Mutiny on the Bounty* (1935), *A Night at the Opera* (1935), *Romeo and Juliet* (1936), *The Good Earth* (1937), *Camille* (1937)—the last two of which were released after his death.

While Fitzgerald was writing *The Last Tycoon* he drafted an inscription "To Write in Copy to Shearer":

DEAR NORMA:

You told me you read little because of your eyes but I think this book will interest you—and though the story is purely imaginary perhaps you could see it as an attempt to preserve something of Irving[.] My own impression of him shortly recorded but very dazzling in its effect on me, inspired the best part of the character of Stahr—though I have put in somethings drawn from of other men and, inevitably, much of myself.

I invented a tragic story and Irvings life was, of course, not tragic except his struggle against ill health, because no one has ever written a tragedy about Hollywood (*a Star is Born* was a pathetic story and often beautiful story but not a tragedy and doomed and heroic things do happen here.

With Old Affection and Gratitude [6]

The first documented meeting between Fitzgerald and Thalberg came in 1927 when Fitzgerald was working for First National on "Lipstick." The thirty-one-year-old novelist and the twenty-seven-

To Write in Copy to Shearer

Dear Norma:
   You told me you read little because of your eyes but I think this book will interest you — perhaps you could see it as an attempt to preserve something of Irving and though the story is purely imaginary and ~~He inspired~~ My own impression of him ~~about but~~ shortly recorded but very dazzling in its effect on me, inspired the best part of the character of Stahr — though I have put in ~~much~~ of other men and, inevitably, much of myself.
   ~~It is a tragic story~~ I invented a tragic story ~~because~~ and ~~Stahrs~~ Irvings life was, of course, not tragic except his struggle against ill health, because no one has now written a tragedy about Hollywood and often beautiful story but not a tragedy a Star is Born was a pathetic story, and doomed and heroic things do happen here.
   ~~Stay~~   With old affection and Gratitude

Inscription for Norma Shearer Thalberg.—F. Scott Fitzgerald Papers, Princeton University Library year-old producer talked briefly, and some twelve years later Fitzgerald wrote a memo to himself about the impression Thalberg had made on him:

> We sat in the old commissary at Metro and he said, "Scottie, supposing there's got to be a road through a mountain—a railroad and two or three surveyors and people come to you and you believe some of then and some of them you don't believe; but all in all, there seems to be half a dozen possible roads through those mountains each one of which, so far as you can determine, is as good as the other. Now suppose you happen to be the top man, there's a point where you don't exercise the faculty of judgment in the ordinary way, but simply the faculty of arbitrary decision. You say, 'Well, I think we will put the road there,' and you trace it with you finger and you know in your secret heart and no one else knows, that you have no reason for putting the road there rather than in several other different courses, but you're the only person that knows that you don't know why you're doing it and You've got to stick to that and you've got to pretend that you know and that you did it for specific reasons, even though you're utterly assailed by doubts at times as to the wisdom of your decision because all these other possible decisions keep echoing in your ear. But when you're planning a new enterprise on a grand scale, the people under you mustn't ever know or guess that you're in any doubt because they've all got to have something to look up to and they mustn't ever dream that you're in doubt about any decision. Those things keep occurring."
>
> At that point, some other people came into the commissary and sat down and first thing I knew there was a group of four and the intimacy of the conversation was broken, but I was very much impressed by the shrewdness of what he said—something more than shrewdness—by the largeness of what he thought and how he reached it at the age of 26 which he was then.[7]

The next recorded encounter between the two men came in November–December 1931 when Fitzgerald was employed by MGM to write a screenplay based on Katharine Brush's *Red Headed Woman*, on which Fitzgerald was teamed with another writer, Marcel de Sano. Although Fitzgerald wanted to ask Thalberg—now his boss—to let him work alone, he was dissuaded by studio friends. The Fitzgerald-de Sano screenplay was not used; and Fitzgerald believed that MGM held it against him when he returned to his family in Montgomery, though he had been hired for only five weeks. A now-legendary episode occurred during this 1931 Hollywood stint when, inspired by alcohol, Fitzgerald made himself ridiculous by performing a humorous song at the Thalbergs' home. The next day he received this telegram: "I THOUGHT YOU WERE ONE OF THE MOST AGREEABLE PERSONS AT OUR TEA=NORMA THALBERG." [8] These events were written into "Crazy Sunday," Fitzgerald's 1932 story about Hollywood.

It is possible that Fitzgerald developed a certain resentment toward Thalberg during his work for MGM in 1931. Fitzgerald was just another employee, assigned against his will to collaborate with a writer he regarded as a hack. He did not know whether other writers were assigned to the same project, and he had no control over his own work. This factory system for screenwriters had been developed by Thalberg. Some resentment is discernible in "Crazy Sunday," which presents a mixed assessment of the Thalbergs as Miles Calman and Stella Walker. (The echoes in the name sounds—Stella Walker / Norma Shearer; Calman / Thalberg—provide a clue to identification.) Calman is described as "the only American-born director with both an interesting temperament and an artistic conscience," but the neurotic depiction of him is not totally admiring. Yet after Calman's death in a plane crash—the same death Fitzgerald planned for Stahr—the narrator thinks, "What a hell of a hole he leaves in this damn wilderness—already!" The portrait of Stella Walker Calman is even more ambivalent, if intended as a compliment to Norma Shearer Thalberg, for Stella is a shallow creature whose personality has been created by her husband. After she learns of Calman's death she wants to sleep with the narrator as a way of denying the reality of her husband's death—that is, she feels that by being unfaithful to Calman she can pretend that he is still alive.

It is always risky to read Fitzgerald's fiction as straight biography or autobiography. The Calmans externally resemble the Thalbergs, but their characters are all invented. Indeed, Sheilah Graham reports that Fitzgerald said Miles Calman was actually based on director King Vidor, who was being divorced from actress Eleanor Boardman while Fitzgerald was at MGM in 1931.[9] Fitzgerald's own comment on the sources for "Crazy Sunday" came in a 1935 letter to his agent, Harold Ober: "Do you remember how the Hearst publicity men killed my story 'Crazy Sunday' for *Cosmopolitan*. That was in case someone should get hurt, that it might offend Norma Shearer, Thalberg, John Gilbert or Marion Davies, etc. etc. As a matter of fact I had mixed up those characters so thoroughly that there was no character who could have been identified except possibly King Vidor and he would have been very amused by the story." [10]

Fitzgerald was not in Hollywood during the summer of 1935, the time of his novel. In the summer of 1937 Fitzgerald made his third trip to Hollywood. Deeply in debt and no longer able to write the *Saturday Evening Post* stories that had provided the basis for his income, he had ambitious plans for his new career. Writing to his daughter Scottie en route to Hollywood, he reviewed his previous movie ventures: "I want to profit by these two experiences—I must be very tactful but keep my hand on the wheel from the start—find out the key man among the bosses and the most malleable among the collaborators—then fight the rest tooth and nail until, in fact or in effect, I'm alone on the picture. That's the only way I can do my best work. Given a break I can make them double this contract in less two years." [11]

On 14 July 1937, shortly after his arrival in Hollywood, Fitzgerald met Sheilah Graham at Robert Benchley's Garden of Allah apartment. They fell in love and established a relationship that endured for the rest of Fitzgerald's life—with interruptions caused by his drinking bouts. *The Last Tycoon* owes at least two debts to Miss Graham: she provided an atmosphere of regularity that made it possible for Fitzgerald to write, and she was the model for Kathleen. [12]

Fitzgerald went to MGM in 1938 with a six-month contract at $1000 per week, which was renewed for a year at $1250. After a polish job on *A Yank at Oxford*, he was given a good assignment to work on Erich Maria Remarque's *Three Comrades* for producer Joseph Mankiewicz. However, Fitzgerald and his collaborator, E. E. Paramore, began feuding; and Fitzgerald was outspokenly angry when Mankiewicz revised the script. Nonetheless, *Three Comrades* was a success, and brought Fitzgerald his only screen credit. Then he worked on several abortive projects—*Infidelity*, *The Women*, *Madame Curie*, *Marie Antoinette*—for producer Hunt Stromberg until his contract option was dropped by MGM in January 1939. Thereafter he free-lanced.

Readers who take *The Last Tycoon* as a roman à clef about Irving Thalberg diminish it. Fitzgerald's note for Norma Shearer stipulated that Thalberg "inspired the best part of the character of Stahr," but the rest came from other men—"and inevitably much of myself." Stahr is a wish-fulfillment, an imaginative projection by Fitzgerald the unsuccessful screenwriter who went to Hollywood in 1937 hoping to become a producer.

Stahr's sense of loss and his attempt to secure a new love are obvious reflections of Fitzgerald's situation. The dead Minna is the hopelessly disturbed Zelda. Kathleen Moore is obviously based on Sheilah Graham. Just as Stahr is struck by Kathleen's resemblance to his Minna, Sheilah Graham resembled Zelda. At the time Fitzgerald first saw Miss Graham—who, like Kathleen, was wearing a silver belt—she was engaged to the Marquis of Donegall, a circumstance Fitzgerald elevated into Kathleen's liaison with a king. Miss Graham's education in Fitzgerald's "college of one" also parallels Kathleen's experience. Finally, Stahr's hesitation about marrying Kathleen is a reflection of Fitzgerald's inability to marry Sheilah Graham.

Pat Brady was obviously based on Louis B. Mayer, though more in terms of Mayer's position at MGM than his personality. The circumstance that Brady is Irish whereas Mayer was a Jew may suggest that Brady was partly inspired by Eddie Mannix, an Irish MGM executive. Like Brady, Mannix had once worked in an amusement park.

Many of the minor characters were drawn from actual Hollywood figures. It seems likely that Jacques La Borwitz was meant to suggest Joseph Mankiewicz, whom Fitzgerald never forgave for rewriting the *Three Comrades* screenplay. One of the notes for the novel reads: "La Borwitz. Joe Mank—pictures smell of rotten bananas." (Fitzgerald seems responsible for changing the spelling from *La Borwits* to *La Borwitz* in the latest typescripts.) Johnny

Swanson was Harry Carey. Robinson was based on Otto Lovering, the assistant director in *Winter Carnival*; the identification is confirmed in two of Fitzgerald's character lists. Mike Van Dyke was based on Robert (Hoppie) Hopkins, a veteran MGM gagman. Boxley was probably Aldous Huxley, who was in Hollywood with Fitzgerald. Jane Meloney may have been suggested by screenwriter Bess Meredyth, with something of Dorothy Parker. Rienmund was possibly based on MGM producer Hunt Stromberg, for whom Fitzgerald had worked.

Although Fitzgerald had earned some $90,000 in eighteen months at MGM, he was characteristically in need of money at the end of his contract and began working at freelance assignments. In February 1939 he made the disastrous Dartmouth trip with Budd Schulberg to work on *Winter Carnival* for producer Walter Wanger of United Artists—and was fired for drunkenness. Schulberg's fictionalized account of the *Winter Carnival* debacle is in his novel, *The Disenchanted* (New York: Random House, 1951). Schulberg, the son of B. P. Schulberg, the former production head at Paramount, was a mine of information about Hollywood. One of the reasons why Fitzgerald and Schulberg did not do their work on *Winter Carnival* was that they were having long conversations about Hollywood.[13] Fitzgerald wanted to know about B. P. Schulberg's working habits and how they compared with Thalberg's. At this time Budd Schulberg did not know that Fitzgerald was planning a Hollywood novel. When he let Schulberg read the opening chapters of *The Last Tycoon* in 1940, Fitzgerald remarked, "I sort of combined you with my daughter Scottie for Cecilia."[14] Scottie was nineteen and a student at Vassar. Although Fitzgerald and Scottie were in conflict over her attitude toward her studies and he was writing her a series of severe letters, he nonetheless believed that he felt her world intensely. It was therefore virtually automatic for Fitzgerald to project Scottie into Cecelia—adding the inside knowledge and the attitude of the Hollywood child he gleaned from Schulberg. At the time Fitzgerald was working on the novel, Schulberg was writing his own Hollywood novel, *What Makes Sammy Run?* Schulberg had not known that he and Fitzgerald were, in a sense, competing, but he was not resentful when he read *The Last Tycoon*. Schulberg recalls: "It was a complex moment because he had just finished reading 'Sammy,' had encouraged me with his praise, and had volunteered to write a letter to Bennett Cerf that could be used on the jacket. By this time I had known so many writers that I realized how they fed on one another." [15]

3 /

Preparation and

Composition

SCREENWRITING NEVER SATISFIED FITZGERALD—EVEN AT $1250 per week—and in 1938 he began writing Maxwell Perkins about two possible book projects: a "modern novel" and an expansion of the four medieval "Count of Darkness" stories.[1] On 4 January 1939—after he knew that MGM would not renew his contract— Fitzgerald wrote Perkins about his writing plans for 1939: "if periods of three or four months are going to be possible in the next year or so I would much rather do a modern novel. One of those novels that can only be written at the moment and when one is full of the idea. . . . I think it would be a quicker job to write a novel like that between 50 and 60,000 words long than to do a thorough revision job with an addition of 15,000 words on 'Phillipe.' " [2]

In April 1939 Fitzgerald took Zelda on a disastrous trip to Cuba, and ended up drying out in a New York hospital. At this time he discussed his writing plans with Maxwell Perkins, Harold Ober, and Charles Scribner. The earliest clear evidence that Fitzgerald was working on the novel that became *The Last Tycoon* is in his 22 May 1939 letter to Perkins, five months after the termination of his MGM contract, although the purpose of this letter was to insist that he was *not* writing a Hollywood novel: "Just had a letter from Charlie Scribner. . . . He seemed under the full conviction that the novel was about Hollywood and I am in terror that this mis-information may have been disseminated to the literary columns. If I ever gave any such impression it is entirely false: I said that the novel was about some things that had happened to me in the last two years. It is distinctly *not* about Hollywood (and if it were it is the last impression that I would want to get about.)" ³ The novel was, of course, about Hollywood; but Fitzgerald was concerned that an announcement of his material would make it difficult for him to find movie work. A week later Fitzgerald informed Ober of his plans.

> *First, I have* blocked out my novel completely with a rough sketch of every episode and event and character so that under proper circumstances I could begin writing it tomorrow. It is a short novel about fifty thousand words long and should take me three to four months.
>
> However, for reasons of income tax I feel I should be more secure before I launch into such a venture—*but* it will divide easily into five thousand word lengths and *Collier's* might take a chance on it where the *Post* would not. They might at least be promised a first look at it when it's finished—possibly some time late in the Fall.⁴

The idea that *Collier's* might be interested in serializing the novel resulted from the circumstance that in May 1939 Fitzgerald had satisfactorily revised an old story, "Thumbs Up," for *Collier's* and had corresponded with Kenneth Littauer, the fiction editor, about a story Sheilah Graham had written.

In July 1939 Ober declined to make an advance against an unsold story, and Fitzgerald broke with him. There is no further correspondence between them about the novel, and Fitzgerald pressed Perkins into service as his New York spokesman in his dealings with Littauer. On 18 July Fitzgerald wrote to Littauer proposing an advance of $750 for first refusal on the novel and some short stories.

> I was of course delighted to finish off the Civil War story ["Thumbs Up"] to your satisfaction at last—I may say to my satisfaction also, because the last version *felt* right. And after twenty months of moving pictures it was fun to be back at prose writing again. That has been the one bright spot in a situation you may have heard of from Harold Ober: that I have been laid up and writing in bed since the first of May, and I am only just up and dressed.
>
> As I told your Mr. Wilkinson when he telephoned, the first thing

I did when I had to quit pictures for awhile was to block out my novel (a short one the size of *Gatsby*) and made the plan on a basis of 2500 word units. The block-out is to be sure that I can take it up or put it down in as much time as is allowed between picture work and short stories. I will never again sign a long picture contract, no matter *what* the inducement: most of the profit when one overworks goes to doctors and nurses.

Meanwhile I am finishing a 4500 word piece designed for your pages. It should go off to you airmail Saturday night, because I am going back to the studios for a short repair job Monday.

I would like to send the story *directly to you,* which amounts to a virtual split with Ober. This is regrettable after twenty years of association but it had better be masked under the anonymity of "one of those things." Harold is a fine man and has been a fine agent and the fault is mine. Through one illness he backed me with a substantial amount of money (all paid back to him now with Hollywood gold), but he is not prepared to do that again with growing boys to educate—and failing this, I would rather act for a while as my own agent in the short story, just as I always have with Scribner's. But I much prefer, both for his sake and mine, that my sending you the story direct should be a matter *between you and me.* For the fact to reach him through your office might lead to an unpleasant rather than a pleasant cleavage of an old relationship. I am writing him *later in the week* making the formal break on terms that will be understood between us, and I have no doubt that in some ways he will probably welcome it. Relationships have an unfortunate way of wearing out, like most things in this world.

Would you be prepared, in return for an agreement or contract for *first look at the novel* and at *a specified number of short stories in a certain time,* to advance me $750., by wire on receipt of this letter—which will be even before the story reaches you Monday? This is a principal factor in the matter at the moment as these three months of illness have got me into a mess with income tax and insurance problems. When you get this will you wire me Yes or No, because if you can't, I can probably start studio work Friday. This may be against your general principles—from my angle I am offering you rather a lot for no great sum.

P.S. If this meets your favorable consideration the money should be wired to the Bank of America, Culver City. If not would you wire me an answer anyhow because my determination to handle my magazine relationship myself is quite final.

The novel will be just short of 50,000 words.[5]

Littauer's reply has not been located, but he obviously rejected Fitzgerald's proposition. (Some of the gaps in the Fitzgerald/Littauer correspondence can be accounted for by telephone calls.) The short story has not been identified, but was probably "Discard," which Littauer declined on 28 July as "too elliptical or something." During the summer and fall of 1939 Fitzgerald unsuccessfully submitted other stories to *Collier's*, of which only "Three Hours Between Planes" and "Mike Van Dyke's Christmas Wish" are named; but it seems likely that "Last Kiss" was also submitted. The time when "Last Kiss" was written cannot be determined—ironically, it was finally published by *Collier's* in 1949—but it has a significant relationship to the material of the novel. Although the hero is a producer, he is nothing like Stahr; however, the heroine resembles Sheilah Graham and anticipates Kathleen. Like Kathleen and Miss Graham, Sybil Higgins is an English girl with an unusual background—she admits to having been "an old man's darling." The mood of "Last Kiss" is tragic, for Sybil is defeated by Hollywood and dies.

In June 1939 Fitzgerald told Zelda that he had "blocked out a novel," but not until 31 October did he inform Scottie that he was writing a novel, being careful to tell her nothing about the material.

Look! I have begun to write something that is maybe great, and I'm going to be absorbed in it four or six months. It may not *make* us a cent but it will pay expenses and it is the first labor of love I've undertaken since the first part of *Infidelity*. . . .

Anyhow I am alive again—getting by that October did something—with all its strains and necessities and humiliations and struggles. I don't drink. I am not a great man, but sometimes I think the impersonal and objective quality of my talent and the sacrifices of it, in pieces, to preserve its essential value has some sort of epic grandeur. Anyhow after hours I nurse myself with delusions of that sort.

And I think when you read this book, which will encompass the time when you knew me as an adult, you will understand how intensively I knew your world—not *ex*tensively because I was so ill and unable to get about.[6]

The first dated synopsis for the novel was sent to Littauer (with copy to Perkins) on 29 September 1939.

This will be difficult for two reasons. First that there is one fact about my novel, which, if it were known, would be immediately and unscrupulously plagiarized by the George Kaufmans, etc., of this world. Second, that I live always in deadly fear that I will take the edge off an idea for myself by summarizing or talking about it in advance. But, with these limitations, here goes:
The novel will be fifty thousand words long. As I will have to write sixty thousand words to make room for cutting I have figured it as a four months job—three months for the writing—one month for revision. The thinking, according to my conscience and the evidence of sixty pages of outline and notes, *has already been done.* I would infinitely rather do it, now that I am well again, than take hack jobs out here.

The Story occurs during four or five months in the year 1935. It is told by Cecelia,* the daughter of a producer named Bradogue in Hollywood. Cecelia is a pretty, modern girl neither good nor bad, tremendously human. Her father is also an important character. A shrewd man, a gentile, and a scoundrel of the lowest variety. A self-made man, he has brought up Cecelia to be a princess, sent her East to college, made of her rather a snob, though, in the course of the story, her character evolves *away from this,* That is, she was twenty when the events that she tells occurred, but she is twenty-five when

---

* Fitzgerald consistently spelled this name *Cecelia.* His form has been retained in this study—except when quoting from Edmund Wilson's edition of *The Last Tycoon,* where it was emended to *Cecilia.* The character was named for Fitzgerald's cousin, Cecilia Delihant Taylor, whom he addressed as "Cousin Ceci." It is impossible to determine whether Fitzgerald simply didn't know the correct spelling for *Cecilia,* or whether the spelling *Cecelia* was deliberate. Fitzgerald's spellings for the names of his characters have been followed in this study. His spelling inconsistencies and idiosyncracies have been preserved when quoting the manucripts.

she tells about the events, and of course many of them appear to her in a different light.

Cecelia is the narrator because I think I know exactly how such a person would react to my story. She is *of* the movies but not *in* them. She probably was born the day "The Birth of a Nation" was pre-viewed and Rudolf Valentino came to her fifth birthday party. So she is, all at once, intelligent, cynical but understanding and kindly toward the people, great or small, who are of Hollywood.

She focuses our attention upon two principal characters—Milton Stahr (who is Irving Thalberg—and *this is my great secret*) and Thalia, the girl he loves. Thalberg has always fascinated me. His peculiar charm, his extraordinary good looks, his bountiful success, the tragic end of his great adventure. The events I have built around him are fiction, but all of them are things which might very well have hap-pened, and I am pretty sure that I saw deep enough into the character of the man so that his reactions are authentically what they would have been in life. So much so that he may be recognized—but it will also be recognized that *no single fact is actually true*. For example, in my story he is unmarried or a widower, leaving out completely any complication with Norma.

In the beginning of the book I want to pour out my whole impres-sion of this man Stahr as he is seen during an airplane trip from New York to the coast—of course, through Cecelia's eyes. She has been hopelessly in love with him for a long time. She is never going to win anything more from him than an affectionate regard, even that tainted by his dislike of her father (parallel the deadly dislike of each other between Thalberg and Louis B. Mayer). Stahr is over-worked and deathly tired, ruling with a radiance that is almost moribund in its phosphorescence. He has been warned that his health is under-mined, but being afraid of nothing the warning is unheeded. He has had everything in life except the privilege of giving himself unselfishly to another human being. This he finds on the night of a semi-serious earthquake (like in 1935) a few days after the opening of the story.

It has been a very full day even for Stahr—the bursted water mains, which cover the whole ground space of the lot to the depth of several feet, seems to release something in him. Called over to the outer lot to supervise the salvation of the electrical plant (for like Thalberg, he has a finger in every pie of the vast bakery) he finds two women stranded on the roof of a property farmhouse and goes to their rescue.

Thalia Taylor is a twenty-six year old widow, and my present conception of her should make her the most glamorous and sympathetic of my heroines. Glamorous in a new way because I am in secret agreement with the public in detesting the type of feminine arrogance that has been pushed into prominence in the case of Brenda Frazier, etc. People simply do not sympathize deeply with those who have had *all* the breaks, and I am going to dower this girl, like Rosalba in Thackeray's "Rose in the Ring" with "a little misfortune." She and the woman with her (to whom she is serving as companion) have come secretly on the lot through the other woman's curiosity. They have been caught there when the catastrophe occurred.

Now we have a love affair between Stahr and Thalia, an immediate, dynamic, unusual, physical love affair—and I will write it so that you can publish it. At the same time I will send you a copy of how it will appear in book form somewhat stronger in tone.

This love affair is the meat of the book—though I am going to treat it, remember, as it comes through to Cecelia. That is to say by making Cecelia at the moment of her telling the story, an intelligent and observant woman, I shall grant myself the privilege, as Conrad did, of letting her imagine the actions of the characters. Thus, I hope to get the verisimilitude of a first person narrative, combined with a Godlike knowledge of all events that happen to my characters.

Two events beside the love affair bulk large in the intermediary chapters. There is a definite plot on the part of Bradogue, Cecelia's father, to get Stahr out of the company. He has even actually and factually considered having him murdered. Bradogue is the monopolist at its worst—Stahr, in spite of the inevitable conservatism of the self-made man, is a paternalistic employer. Success came to him young, at twenty-three, and left certain idealisms of his youth unscarred. Moreover, he is a worker. Figuratively he takes off his coat and pitches in, while Bradogue is not interested in the making of pictures save as it will benefit his bank account.

The second incident is how young Cecelia herself, in her desperate love for Stahr, throws herself at his head. In her reaction at his indifference she gives herself to a man whom she does not love. This episode is *not* absolutely necessary to the serial. It could be tempered but it might be best to eliminate it altogether.

Back to the main theme, Stahr cannot bring himself to marry Thalia. It simply doesn't seem part of his life. He doesn't realize that she has become necessary to him. Previously his name has been associated with this or that well-known actress or society personality and Thalia is poor, unfortunate, and tagged with a middle class exterior which doesn't fit in with the grandeur Stahr demands of life. When she realizes this she leaves him temporarily, leaves him not because he has no legal intentions toward her but because of the hurt of it, the remainder of a vanity from which she had considered herself free.

Stahr is now plunged directly into the fight to keep control of the company. His health breaks down very suddenly while he is on a trip to New York to see the stockholders. He almost dies in New York and comes back to find that Bradogue has seized upon his absence to take steps which Stahr considers unthinkable. He plunges back into work again to straighten things out.

Now, realizing how much he needs Thalia, things are patched up between them. For a day or two they are ideally happy. They are going to marry, but he must make one more trip East to clinch the victory which he has conciliated in the affairs of the company.

Now occurs the final episode which should give the novel its quality—and its unusualness. Do you remember about 1933 when a transport plane was wrecked on a mountain-side in the Southwest, and a Senator was killed? The thing that struck me about it was that the country people rifled the bodies of the dead. That is just what happens to this plane which is bearing Stahr from Hollywood. The angle is that of three children who, on a Sunday picnic, are the first to discover the wreckage. Among those killed in the accident besides Stahr are two other characters we have met. (I have not been able to go into the minor characters in this short summary.) Of the three children, two boys and a girl, who find the bodies, one boy rifled Stahr's possessions; another, the body of a ruined ex-producer; and the girl, those of a moving picture actress. The possessions which the children find, symbolically determine their attitude toward their act of theft. The possessions of the moving picture actress tend the young girl to a selfish possessiveness; those of the unsuccessful producer sway one of the boys toward an irresolute attitude; while the boy who finds Stahr's briefcase is the one who, after a week, saves and redeems all three by going to a local judge and making full confession.

The story swings once more back to Hollywood for its finale. During the story *Thalia has never once been inside a studio.* After Stahr's death as she stands in front of the great plant which he created, she realizes now that she never will. She knows only that he loved her and that he was a great man and that he died for what he believed in.

This is a novel—not even faintly of the propoganda type. Indeed, Thalberg's opinions were entirely different from mine in many respects that I will not go into. I've long chosen him for a hero (this has been in my mind for three years) because he is one of the half-dozen men I have known who were built on the grand scale. That it happens to coincide with a period in which the American Jews are somewhat uncertain in their morale, is for me merely a fortuitous coincidence. The racial angle shall scarcely be touched on at all. Certainly if Ziegfield could be made into an epic figure than what about Thalberg who was literally everything that Ziegfield wasn't?

There's nothing that worries me in the novel, nothing that seems uncertain. Unlike *Tender is the Night* it is not the story of deterioration—it is not depressing and not morbid in spite of the tragic ending. If one book could ever be "like" another I should say it is more "like" *The Great Gatsby* than any other of my books. But I hope it will be entirely different—I hope it will be something new, arouse new emotions perhaps even a new way of looking at certain phenomena. I have set it safely in a period of five years ago to obtain detachment, but now that Europe is tumbling about our ears this also seems to be for the best. It is an escape into a lavish, romantic past that perhaps will not come again into our time. It is certainly a novel I would like to read. Shall I write it? [7]

The letter sent to Littauer and the copy sent to Perkins have not been located. A four-page carbon copy—with the bottom of page four torn off—is with the notes for *The Last Tycoon*. Another carbon of page four has Fitzgerald's note "Orig Sent thru here" after "Shall I write it?" The rest of page four reads:

As I said, I would rather do this for a minimum price than continue this in-and-out business with the moving pictures where the
rewards are great, but the satisfaction unsatisfactory and the income
tax always mopping one up after the battle.

The minimum I would need to do this with peace of mind would
be $15,000., payable $3000. in advance and $3000. on the first of
November, the first of December, the first of January and the first of
February, on delivery of the last installment. For this I would guaran-
tee to do no other work, specifically pictures, to make any changes in
the manuscript (but not to having them made for me) and to begin
to deliver the copy the first of November, that is to give you fifteen
thousand words by that date.

Unless these advances are compatible with your economy, Kenneth, the deal would be financially impossible for me under the
present line up. Four months of sickness completely stripped me and
until your telegram came I had counted on a buildup of many months
work here before I could *consider* beginning the novel. Once again
a telegram would help tremendously, as I am naturally on my toes
and [*The rest of the letter is missing.*]

Fitzgerald either decided that the $15,000 figure was too low or
that he wanted to have Littauer make the opening bid. In any case,
Fitzgerald later declined to write the serial for $ 15,000.

The 29 September synopsis represents an early form of the
story—without the double blackmail and murder plots, or Kathleen's past as the mistress of a king and her commitment to marry
another man. Of particular significance is Fitzgerald's analysis of
the narrator. Although he compares this novel to *The Great Gatsby*,
it is clear—from both the synopsis and the sections he wrote—that
Fitzgerald intended a more flexible role for Cecelia than he had per-
mitted Nick Carraway. Nick either witnesses or documents every
scene in the novel (except Gatsby's murder); but Cecelia was to be
allowed "to imagine the actions of the characters"—thereby provid-
ing the double viewpoint of narrator and omniscient author.

Littauer responded on 10 October, saying that *Collier's* could
not make an advance without seeing a "substantial sample of the
finished product"—15,000 words.[8] If the sample was sufficiently

promising, *Collier's* was prepared to advance $5,000, with a second advance of $5,000 for the next 20,000 words— "against a total purchase price which remains to be negotiated." Littauer suggested that the purchase price be based on the rate of $2,500 per 7,000– 8,000-word installment, with a bonus of $5,000. Therefore the talking figure for serial rights to a 50,000-word novel was at least $20,000. But *Collier's* was not prepared to consider an advance before seeing a 15,000-word sample, and Fitzgerald needed an advance with which to write the sample. Fitzgerald then wired Perkins to negotiate with Littauer for him. On 16 October 1939 Perkins wrote a memo for Charles Scribner indicating his concern that Fitzgerald would turn to Scribners for backing.

Collier's are quite keen about Scott's idea, but they have a natural suspicion of his reliability. They are willing to pay him approximately $30,000 for the serial if they agree to take it after seeing 15,000 words.—And if they do see that number of words, and if they like them, they will advance him two installments of $5,000 each. The trouble is Scott has such extravagant ideas of what he needs that he says he must have $3,000 a month. I am afraid he will now turn to us to help him do the 15,000. I believe he could on this present basis turn to Harold Ober, whose debt he has entirely cleared up, and who has made plenty of money out of his movie contracts, etc. too. Harold refused to lend him any more, thinking it would do him good, and this made Scott mad, and all this new plan is supposed to be a complete secret from Harold. [9]

While these negotiations were going on—by letter, wire, and phone—Fitzgerald sent Littauer a story called "Mike Van Dyke's Christmas Wish," which was declined because it was "not a rounded short story." [10] Fitzgerald changed the character's name to Pat Hobby, and wrote seventeen sketches about him for *Esquire* in 1939 and 1940. At $250 each, Pat Hobby helped finance the writing of *The Last Tycoon*.

The Pat Hobby stories, which appeared in *Esquire* from January 1940 to May 1941 are uneven, and their relationship to *The Last Tycoon* has been distorted by readers who see them as a quasi-autobiographical account of Fitzgerald in Hollywood. About the only thing that these stories have in common with the novel is the Hollywood setting; the intention, the tone, the themes, are entirely different. Fitzgerald did not write the Pat Hobby series until after he had started work on *The Last Tycoon,* and he wrote them only for money—using Hobby to finance Stahr. It is obvious that Fitzgerald was careful not to waste any *Last Tycoon* material on the Hobby stories. One way he was able to keep the two projects distinct while working on both simultaneously was by sharply differentiating his attitude toward the characters. Pat Hobby is contemptible; Monroe Stahr is heroic. Rarely did Fitzgerald allow Hobby to be sympathetic—as in "Two Old Timers" and "A Patriotic Short." Elsewhere Pat is ignorant, mean, and dishonest. Because critics and students have been conditioned to regard Hollywood as a concentration camp for writers, judgments of the Hobby stories have been influenced by presuppositional responses to Hobby—and Fitzgerald—as victims of Hollywood. But Hobby is only a victim of his own dishonesty and lack of ability.

The Pat Hobby stories were simply an undemanding way to make a little money—$4,250—while Fitzgerald was saving himself for work on *The Last Tycoon.* It is absurd to regard Pat Hobby as a self-portrait of Fitzgerald. Hobby is an illiterate who never had any talent—a cliché-infested dope—with whom Fitzgerald did not identify. Fitzgerald can be connected to Hobby only by viewing Hobby as Fitzgerald's self-warning—an exaggerated depiction of what Fitzgerald was afraid of becoming. Even if Fitzgerald identified with Hobby, then he was using Hobby to dissipate resentments that he did not want to intrude into the novel. The only viewpoint that *The Last Tycoon* and the Hobby stories have in common is contempt for the incompetents.

Fitzgerald fulfilled Perkins' prophecy on 20 October 1939, asking if Scribners could subvene the writing of "the first ten thousand words:"

I have your telegram but meanwhile I found that Collier's proposition was less liberal than I had expected. They want to pay $15,000. for the serial. But (without taking such steps as reneging on my income tax, letting go my life insurance for its surrender value, taking Scottie from college and putting Zelda in a public asylum) I couldn't

last four months on that. Certain debts have been run up so that the larger part of the $15,000. has been, so to speak, spent already. A contraction of my own living expenses to the barest minimum, that is to say a room in a boarding house, abandonment of all medical attention (I still see a doctor once a week) would still leave me at the end not merely penniless but even more in debt than I am now.[11]

On the same day that he wrote to Perkins, Fitzgerald wrote to Littauer reviewing the terms of the proposition:

I was disappointed in our conversation the other day—I am no good on long distance and should have had notes in my hand.

I want to make plain how my proposition differs from yours. First there is the question of the *total* payment; second, the *terms* of payment, which would enable me to finish it in these straightened circumstances.

In any case I shall probably attack the novel. I have about decided to make a last liquidation of assets, put my wife in a public place, and my daughter to work and concentrate on it—simply take a furnished room and live on canned goods.

But writing it under such conditions I should want to market it with the chance of getting a higher price for it.

It was to avoid doing all this, that I took you up on the idea of writing it on installments. I too had figured on the same price per installment you had paid for a story, but I had no idea that you would want to pack more into an installment than your five thousand word maximum for a story. So the fifty thousand words at $2500. for each 5000 word installment would have come to $25,000. In addition, I had figured that a consecutive story is *easi*er rather than harder to write than the same number of words divided into short stories because the characters and settings are determined in advance, so my idea had been to ask you $20,000. for the whole job. But $15,000.—that would be much too marginal. It would be better to write the whole thing in poverty and freedom of movement with the finished product. Fifteen thousand would leave me more in debt than I am now.

On the question of the terms of payment, my proposition was to include the exact amount which you offer in your letter only I had divided it, so that the money would come in batches of $3000. every four weeks, or something like that.

When we had our first phone conversation the fact that I did not have enough to start on, further complicated the matter; I have hoped that perhaps that's where Scribner's would come in. A telegram from Max told me he was going to see you again but I've heard nothing further.

I hope that this will at least clear up any ambiguity. If the proposition is all off, I am very sorry. I regret now that I did not go on with the novel last April when I had some money, instead of floundering around with a lot of disassociated ideas that were half-heartedly attempted and did not really come to anything. I know you are really interested, and thank you for the trouble you have taken.[12]

Like most writers who think of themselves as good businessmen, Fitzgerald was a bad one. He was spoiling a deal over the question of a payment that could not be resolved until he had submitted a sample. Moreover, Perkins was under the impression that *Collier's* was prepared to go as high as $30,000. The thing for Fitzgerald to do was submit the sample. It was clear that Littauer favored the project, and he had agreed to "shorter installments."[13] On 2 November Littauer made a further concession: "We are willing to make you a small advance on the basis of six thousand words of manuscript in hand—provided, of course, that much of the story seems to us promising."[14]

A key factor in Fitzgerald's negotiations with Littauer was that he wanted an expression of confidence. Fitzgerald always needed money, but at this stage he was also seeking a sign that *Collier's* believed in him. He felt forgotten and worried that his friends had given up on him. Ober's refusal to advance him money on stories had hurt Fitzgerald, and it was apparent that Scribners was not offering to back the new novel. Perkins clearly understood that Fitzgerald expected Scribners to underwrite the novel, but Perkins did not feel that he could justify committing the firm.

At this time Fitzgerald sent a 6,000-word sample to both Littauer and Perkins. The actual material has not been identified, but it is virtually certain that Fitzgerald sent an early draft of the opening of the novel—the plane trip to California. The first chapter is a superb opening for the novel—introducing Stahr and foreshadowing major themes—but it was not an ideal sample *as a sample* to submit because much of what Fitzgerald is doing does not become clear until the reader has absorbed more of the novel. Fitzgerald's case would have been much stronger had he been able to send Littauer the first two chapters, including Stahr's initial encounter with Kathleen during the studio flood. Littauer responded by wire on 28 November: "FIRST SIX THOUSAND PRETTY CRYPTIC THEREFORE DISAPPOINTING. BUT YOU WARNED US THIS MIGHT BE SO. CAN WE DEFER VERDICT UNTIL FURTHER DEVELOPMENT OF STORY? IF IT HAS TO BE NOW IT HAS TO BE NO. REGARDS".[15] Fitzgerald immediately reacted telegraphically. To Littauer: "NO HARD FEELINGS THERE HAS NEVER BEEN AN EDITOR WITH PANTS ON SINCE GEORGE LORIMER" [16]—thereby effectively cutting off further negotiations. To Perkins: "PLEASE RUSH THE COPY AIR MAIL TO SATURDAY EVENING POST ATTENTION JOE BRUAN STOP I GUESS THERE ARE NO GREAT MAGAZINES EDITORS LEFT".[17]

"Joe Bruan" was Joseph Bryan III, an associate editor at the *Post*. Fitzgerald and Bryan had never met or corresponded when Fitzgerald phoned him to ask if he would read a sample of the novel. Bryan was excited by the chance: he had gone to Princeton largely because of reading Fitzgerald and had lived in Fitzgerald's room at 15 University Place. Bryan does not know why Fitzgerald decided to call him, but guesses that their mutual friend Donald Ogden Stewart told Fitzgerald about him. (Stewart has no recollection of this.) When he read the material Bryan was deeply disappointed to find that it was too "broad" for the *Post*. He circulated it to the other editors, but the decision was unanimous: the *Post* could not publish the novel.[18]

Concerned about the effect Littauer's decision would have on Fitzgerald, Perkins wired on the 29 November: "A BEAUTIFUL START. STIRRING AND NEW. CAN WIRE YOU TWO HUNDRED FIFTY AND A THOUSAND BY JANUARY." [19] He was acting in a private capacity, not on behalf of Scribners. Perkins—who was not a rich man—had come into a small inheritance and was prepared to gamble some of it on Fitzgerald. On the same day Fitzgerald wired Perkins to show the synopsis to agent Leland Hayward, with the idea that Hayward could get a movie studio to underwrite his work on the novel in return for the movie rights—a reversal of Fitzgerald's earlier anxiety that the movie people might learn about his novel.[20] Hayward told Perkins that he could not handle the property until it was written.

One of the results of Littauer's decision was that Fitzgerald fell off the wagon temporarily. When *Collier's* editor Max Wilkinson called on him in December 1939 he found Fitzgerald drunk and abusive.[21] On 7 December, Fitzgerald sent Perkins "a little more, introducing the character of the heroine"—part, at least, of Chapter 2.[22] Fitzgerald made no further attempts to deal with *Collier's*; and between the end of 1939 and the fall of 1940 there were no progress reports to Perkins. Nevertheless, *Collier's* appears to have retained an interest in the novel after Fitzgerald broke off negotiations, for on 7 December 1940 he wrote Scottie that he had recently seen Littauer in Los Angeles. On 23 February 1940 Fitzgerald submitted a short-short, "Dearly Beloved" to *Esquire*, which Arnold Gingrich declined.[23] This story marks a stage in the gestation of *The Last Tycoon*, for it is about a Negro who is interested in the Rosicrucians. Although February was too early for Fitzgerald to be working on episode 14 of the novel—where Stahr and Kathleen meet the Negro gathering grunion—the existence of "Dearly Beloved" in February suggests that Fitzgerald had such a character in mind. In March 1940 Fitzgerald took an assignment to adapt "Babylon Revisited" for independent producer Lester Cowan, for which he earned something between $2300 and $5000.[24]

Frances Kroll Ring, Fitzgerald's secretary, reports that he was not able to devote full attention to his novel until after he moved to the Laurel Avenue apartment in May / June 1940. "Concerning the constant revisions of the early chapters of the Last Tycoon: Scott made so many starts before he got into working on the book full time, that he necessarily made changes with each new start. In Encino, he worked mostly on notes interrupted by turning out the Pat Hobby stories for bucks. When he moved to Laurel, he began to work on LT again. This time, the interruption was the Babylon Revisited screenplay. He didn't begin writing the book in a continuous stream until after the screenplay was done." [25] This chronology indicates that Fitzgerald made rapid progress on the novel, writing much of the seventeen episodes in less than six months.

The first evidence of substantial progress on the novel comes in Perkins' 19 September 1940 letter to Fitzgerald expressing pleasure in John O'Hara's report that he had read 25,000 words. A great admirer of Fitzgerald's work, O'Hara told him, "Scott, don't take any more movie jobs till you've finished this. You work so slowly and this is so good, you've got to finish it. It's real Fitzgerald." [26] In the fall of 1940 Fitzgerald stayed on the wagon and worked steadily on the novel, interrupting it only to write an adaptation of Emlyn Williams' *The Light of Heart* for Twentieth Century-Fox in October. From October 1940 Fitzgerald included progress reports in his weekly letters to Zelda: "I expect to be back on my novel any day and this time to finish a two months' job" (11 October); "I'm trying desperately to finish my novel by the middle of December and it's a little like working on "Tender is the Night" at the end—I think of nothing else. . . . My room is covered with charts like it used to be for "Tender is the Night" telling the different movements of the characters and their histories" (19 October); "I am deep in the novel, living in it, and it makes me happy. It is a *constructed* novel like *Gatsby*, with passages of poetic prose when it fits the action, but no ruminations or sideshows like *Tender*. Everything must contribute to the dramatic movement. . . . Two thousand words today and all good" (23 October); "The novel is hard as pulling teeth but that is because it is in its early character-planting phase. I feel people so less intently than I did once that this is harder. It means welding together hundreds of stray impressions and incidents to form the fabric of entire personalities" (2 November); "No news except that the novel progresses and I am angry that this little illness has slowed me up. I've had trouble with my heart before but never anything organic. This is not a major attack but seems to have come on gradually and luckily a cardiogram showed it up in time" (6 December); "The novel is about three-quarters through and I think I can go on till January 12 without doing any stories or going back to the studio. I couldn't go back to the studio anyhow in my present condition as I have to spend most of the time in bed where I write on a wooden desk . . ." (13 December). [27]

To Edmund Wilson—who would edit the novel for posthumous publication—Fitzgerald reported on 25 November 1940: "I think my novel is good. I've written it with difficulty. It is completely upstream in mood and will get a certain amount of abuse but is first hand and I am trying a little harder than I ever have to be exact and honest emotionally. I honestly hoped somebody else would write it but nobody seems to be going to." The letter has a postscript. "This sounds like such a bitter letter—I'd rewrite it except for a horrible paucity of time. Not even time to be bitter." [28]

F. Scott Fitzgerald died of a heart attack on 21 December 1940, leaving 44,000 words of the latest working draft of the novel.

4 /

The Drafts

WHEN FITZGERALD BEGAN WRITING *The Last Tycoon* IN 1939 HE had not worked on a novel for five years; and after 1935 he was no longer able to write the 5,000-word commercial-length short story, a form he had mastered in the twenties. The Fitzgerald/Ober correspondence reveals that the *Post*-type stories Fitzgerald tried to write after *Tender Is the Night* required extraordinary editorial assistance, and that even with such help some were salable only because Fitzgerald's name was on them. During the 1937–40 Hollywood period he published short-shorts in *Esquire*, few of which had any distinction. This form appealed to Fitzgerald because it did not require an extended effort. A short-short of 1,500–2,500 words could be written in one or two sittings, and presented no structural problems, for most of these pieces were expanded anecdotes.

Hollywood did not ruin Fitzgerald as a writer. The prose of *The Last Tycoon* shows no damage to Fitzgerald's style. Nonetheless, it is likely that screenplay work affected his structural powers. The technique of the screenplay is scenic and episodic. The screenwriter is writing for the camera, with the knowledge that the structure and pacing of the movie will be achieved through editing the film. Moreover, many screenwriting assignments are piece-work, requiring the writer to work on individual scenes. It seems clear that Fitzgerald had become accustomed to thinking in episodes by 1939. After Chapter I Fitzgerald was not writing chapters, but episodes for the novel.

The opening of a novel is the hardest part for a writer because it involves building in preparatory material and making decisions about point of view and structure that will affect the rest of the work. Fitzgerald's problems with the first chapters of the novel are instructive. Only when he stopped trying to shape chapters did the writing progress rapidly. Beginning with episode 7 of Chapter 2, Fitzgerald wrote only episodes or sections. (In this study the chapter designations after Chapter 1 refer to the chapters Edmund Wilson assembled from the episodes.) It is too simple to claim that the shift to episodes accounts for the relative speed with which Fitzgerald's work progressed after Chapter 2. There is another factor involved— Fitzgerald's sense of urgency. When he resumed full-time work on the novel in the summer of 1940 after interrupting it for the "Babylon Revisited" screenplay, he had imposed a December deadline on himself. Initially this deadline was determined by finances as well as by his strong desire to re-establish himself as a novelist. But after his first diagnosed heart attack in November 1940 he had a sense that he was writing against the clock. Instead of trying to polish each chapter as it was written, Fitzgerald decided to push through to a complete draft, which he would then rework. All of his life Fitzgerald had been a painstaking reviser, and there is no reason to suppose that he regarded the episodes of this novel as anything more than working drafts.

Fitzgerald's outline-chart for the novel exists in five versions. None of the outlines is dated, but the order can be clearly established on the basis of structural alterations and name changes (e.g., Bradogue [Baird [Brady). The earliest surviving outline is an unrevised typescript headed "(version Y)"—indicating that Fitzgerald regarded it as a preliminary form of the outline. This version breaks the action into 10 chapters but has only 23 episodes. The plot is substantially that of the latest outline, consisting of two interconnected stories—Stahr's love for Kathleen and his struggle with Brady. Fitzgerald estimated the material at 52,500 words. (*The Great Gatsby* has 48,852 words.)

The second outline is a heavily revised typescript which breaks the novel down into 8 chapters and 31 episodes totalling 50,000 words. Beginning with this version Fitzgerald used a 3-column format: a column of episodes; a column indicating a 5-act structure; and a column of commentary.

CHAPTERS   (version Y)

I.	The airplane trip; and Cecelia decides to tell her story	7500
	A. Introduction	
	B. In some stop--Schwartz and Rogers	
	C. With Stahr in Front	
II.	A. Stahr meeting Thalia	2500
	B. Stahr meeting Rogers--Rogers conversation with Stahr	2500
III	Thalia's response to Stahr	2500
IV	Thalia and part of her story	2500
V	How Stahr worked out a picture	5000
	A. Story conference	
	B. Railroad episode and idealism about making non-profit picture	
	C. Stahr's Visit to Sets	
VI	A. Cecelia's seduction and her love for Stahr)	
	B. A good part of Stahr's story)	7500
	C. Cecelia takes her father off guard)	
VII	Stahr and Thalia alone--Stahr's house	5000
VIII	A. Robinson, the Cutter & Dartmouth	2500
	B. Stahr sick in East hears.	
	C. On Coast. The meeting of writers, etc.	2500
	D. Firing of secretaries, technicians, etc.	2500
IX.	A. Stahr's return and anger	
	B. Bradogue Plot	
	C. Stahr's departure to include big scene for Thalia	2500
X	A. The Fall of the Plane	5000
	B. Epilogue in Hollywood	2500
		52,500

Earliest surviving outline-plan.—F. Scott Fitzgerald Papers, Princeton
University Library

Episodes   New Names Based for Dialogue

A. 1. The Plane
2. Nashville
3. Up forward — Johnny Swanson —   6000

B. 4. Prologue – Power – School Meany
5. The Earthquake
6. The Back lot   6000
7. Afterwards (To do with Thalia)

C. 8. Stahr's work and health. From something she wrote
9. Sleeps at studio. The Camera man.
10. Taking the guest around—his story conference
11. The Story Conference — Composing
12. Railway piece — and Idealism about non-profit pictures
13. Visit to Sets. Reinke
14. Second Meeting that night. Small   7600
15. Football game. Celia and Wylie — Try to get on lot
16. Malibu seduction DEAD MIDDLE   5000

D.

E. 17. Celia breaks in on father. Tells Stahr
18. Brady and Stahr – deal that won't jell with Wylie
19. The Cummerband – market
20. Stahr goes with Cecelia – Trocadero Bowl
21. Cecelia and Thalia meet at   6000

F. 22. The Storm breaks Scene Gulf Dawn Underdevelopment
23. Throws over Cecelia. Stops making pictures. Leis could be cut
24. Last fling with Thalia. Old Stavrou brother at Europe

G. 25. Braddock wants to Robinson Smith Blacharten & Cecila. (19 + 20)   8500
26. Sick in Washington To quit?
27. Files and there pros Manix too, Cecelia murder Co
28. Plan and execution at airport. S.G.
29. Thalia at airport. S.G.

H. 30. The Plane falls Tortula (the future in Teenaker
31. The End. Outside the studio. S.G.
32. Harry Garry Johnny Swanson funeral   5500

Camera
26. Stahr keeps plan. Camera man. O.K.
27. Stops it — stay with Celia & Collije.   Aldo

13(a) Celia and Stahr.

Act I ("The Plane")   6,000

Act II (The Circus)   19,000

Act III (The Underworld)   11,000

Act IV (The Murderers)   8,500

Act V (The End)   5,500

59,000

Chapter A. Martha, Cecilia, Stahr, white, Schwartz Jr.

Chapter C is equal to guest bid + Gatsby's party. Throw everything into this.

Chapter B. Introduces Brady & Thalia, Robinson + apartments

Chapter D. Salverini, Smith II

Episodes		Act I	June	Chapter (A). Introduce Cecelia,
A 1. The Plane	*June 28th*	(The Plane)	6,000	Stahr, White, Schwartze.
2. Nashville				
3. Up Forward *Different*		*Stahr*		
	6000			
B 4. Johnny Swanson--Baird-Power-	*July 28th*	Act I¹	*July – early August*	Chapter (B) Introduces Baird,
Sch--K ~~Schaal~~ leaving		(The Circus)	19,000	Thalia, Robinson and secretaries.
				almo—picces of mind — sustain
5. The Earthquake				Chapter (C) is equal to guest
6. The Back lot				list and Gatsby's party. Throw
7. Afterwards (To do with Thalia)	6000			everything into this *with selection.*
				always had a part through leading #13
C 8. Stahr's work and health. From	*July 29th*	*The Movement toward*		Chapter (D) ~~Introduces Smith.~~
something she wrote		*Thalia*		
9. Sleeps at studio. The Camera man.				
10. Taking the guest around--the story				
conference, *first half*				
11. Commissary and Idealism about non-				
profit pictures. *Phone call*				
12. Visit to Sets. ~~Rushes.~~				
13. Second Meeting that night. ~~Sixth.~~	*75 00*			*Three episodes. Atmosphere*
D 13a. Cecelia and Stahr.	*august 6th*			*in 15 most important. Heat*
	7500			*of whole. Fund of the know too*
14. Football game. Cecelia and Wylie *and Wande*				*late*
15. Malibu seduction. Try to get on lot.				
~~DEAD MIDDLE~~				
	5500.			
→ *Schrk arriving.*	*aug 10th*		*aug – early / Sept.*	Chapter (E) *this belongs*
E 16.17 Celia breaks in on father. ~~Talks~~		Act III 11,500		*to the women. It*
~~as Stahr.~~		(The Underworld)		*introduces Smith (for the*
17 21 Baird and Stahr--double blackmail.				*first time? Boating*
Quarrel with Wylie.				
18.16 The Cummerbund - market— *Break of Stahr, Thalia*				
19. Stahr goes with Cecelia - Trocadero	*aug 20th*	*The Struggle*		
or Bowl.				
20. 19 Cecelia and Thalia meet. *+ Fifty.*		6000		
F 21. The Storm breaks at Screen Guild. Dance	*aug 28th*			Chapter (F) *The blows*
	- Sept 14th			*fall on Stahr. Sense of*
22. 21 Sick in Washington. To quit?				*heat all thru, culminating*
~~21 a Story~~ *co—— — half - under - self.*				*in 24*
23. Throws over Cecelia, Stops making pictures.				
Lies low after Cut				
Cecelia talks her father				
24. Last fling with Thalia. Old stars in heat				
wave at Encino.				
	5500			
G 25. Baird gets Smith. Fleishacker and Cecelia.		Act IV	Sept	Chapter G. *The suit and*
(S.G. & Home)		(The Murderers)	8000	*the price.*
26. Stahr hears plan. Camera man, O.K.		*Defeat*		
27. Stops it--very sick. (Cecelia to college;)				
28. Resolve problem. Thalia at airport S.G.		8500		
H 29. The Plane falls. Portents of the future in *Sept*		Act V	Oct	Chapter (H) *Stahr's death*
Fleishacker. *- 6t*		(End)	5500	
30. Outside the studio. S.G.		*Silence*		
31. Johnny Swanson at funeral	5500			
			50,000	

p.s.) Written for two people — for V.S.F. at 17 and for E.W. at 45 — it must please them both.

Third outline-plan.—F. Scott Fitzgerald Papers, Princeton University Library

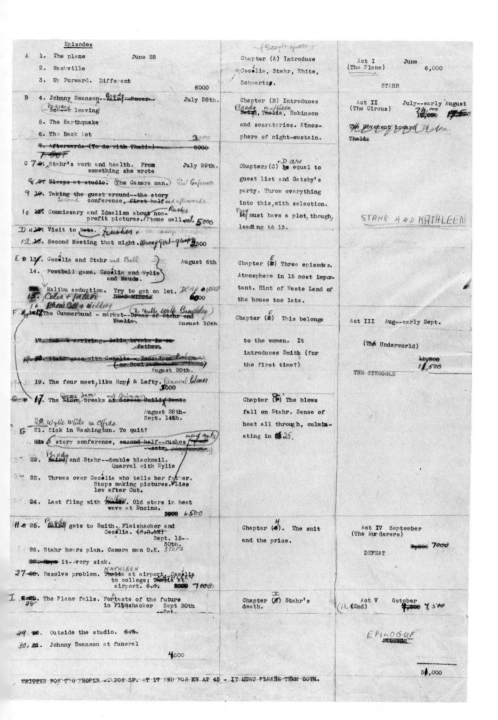

Fourth outline-plan.—F. Scott Fitzgerald Papers, Princeton University Library

Episodes		

A 1. The plane   June 28
2. Nashville
3. Up Forward. Different
         6000
	Chapter (A) Introduce
	Cecelia, Stahr, White,
	Schwartze.
		Act I June
		(THE PLANE)
		      6000
		
		STAHR

B 4. Johnny Swanson--Marcus leaving --Brady July 28th. 5. The Earthquake 6. The Back lot 3000	Chapter (B) Introduces Brady, Kathleen, Robinson and secretaries. Atmos- phere of night-sustain	Act II (THE CIRCUS July--early August 21,000

C 7. The Camera man.   July 29
  Stahr's work and health. From
  something she wrote
8. First Conference
9. Second conference and afterwards.
10. Commissary and Idealism about non-
  profit pictures. Rushes Phone call,
  etc.
        5000
	Chapters (C) & (D) are
	equal to guest list and
	Gatsby's party. Throw
	everything into this, with
	selection. They must have
	a plot, though, leading to
	13
		STAHR AND KATHLEEN

D 11. Visit to rushes.
12. Second Meeting that night.
  Wrong girl--glimpse
      2500		

E 13. Cecelia and Stahr and Ball - Aug. 6th
  Football game. Cecelia and
        Wylie and Maude.
14. Malibu seduction. Try to get on lot.
      DEAD MIDDLE
15. Cecelia and father
16. Phone call & Wedding. 6000
	Chapter (E) Three episodes
	Atmosphere in 15 most
	important. Hint of Waste
	Land of the house too late.	

F 17. The Damn breaks with Brimmer
18. The Cummerbund - market--
    (The theatre with Benchley)
          August 10th
19. The four meet, like Hop and Lefty.
  Renewal. Palomar
20. Wylie White in Office
     August 28th-Sept. 14th.
	Chapter (F) This belongs
	to the women. It introduces
	Smith (for the 1st time?)
		Act III Aug-early
		Sept.
		(The Underworld)
		11,500
		
		THE STRUGGLE

G 21. Sick in Washington. To quit?
22. Brady and Stahr--double blackmail.
    Quarrel with Wylie.
23. Throws over Cecelia who tells her
  father. Stops making pictures.
  A story conference--rushes and
  sets. Lies low after Cut.
24. Last fling with Kathleen. Old
  stars in heat wave at Encino.
 	
      6500
	Chapter (G) The blows
	fall on Stahr. Sense of
	heat all through, culmina-
	ting in 25.	

H 25. Brady gets to Smith. Fleishacker
  and Cecelia. (S.G.&K)
      Sept. 15-30th.
26. Stahr hears plan. Camera man O.K.
  Stops it--very sick.
27. Resolve problem. Thalia at airport.
  Cecelia to college; Thalia at
  airport. S.G.
      7000
	Chapter (H). The suit and
	the price.
		Act IV September
		(The Murderers)
		7000
		DEFEAT

I 28. The Plane falls. Fortaste of the
  future in Flieshacker
     Sept 30th-Oct.
29. Outside the studio. S.G.
30. Johnny Swanson at funeral
    4500
	Chapter (I) Stahr's death.	Act V October
		(The End)
		4500
		
		EPILOGUE

WRITTEN FOR TWO PEOPLE - FOR SF AT 17 AND FOR EW AT 45 - IT MUST PLEASE THEM BOTH   51,000

Final outline-plan.—F. Scott Fitzgerald Papers, Princeton University Library

The third outline—a revised typescript—is an elaboration of the second. The structure is still 8 chapters of 31 episodes; but Fitzgerald added dates indicating the pacing of the action from 28 June to 30 September. At the bottom of this outline-chart Fitzgerald noted in holograph: "Written for two people—for F. S. F. [Scottie Fitzgerald] at 17 and for E. W. [Edmund Wilson] at 45—it must please them both."

In the fourth outline—a revised typescript—Fitzgerald achieved the 9 chapter / 30 episode structure principally by cancelling episode 7 for "Afterwards (To do with Thalia)." This projected episode followed the rescue of the girls in the flood, and the manuscripts show that Fitzgerald originally planned to extend the first meeting between Stahr and Kathleen (Thalia). Episode 17 ("Schenk arriving. Celia breaks in on Father.") and episode 18 ("Stahr goes with Cecelia—Trocadero or Bowl.") were also cancelled; and episode 20 was added ("Wylie White in Office"). The fifth and latest outline is an unrevised typescript of the fourth version.

Edmund Wilson used Fitzgerald's latest outline for the outline printed in *The Last Tycoon*, but he emended it. Wilson omitted from episode 13 the note on "Football game. Cecelia and Wylie and Maude." He changed the dates for episodes 17–18 and 20–21. He deleted the references to S. G.—an obligatory change because Fitzgerald's relationship with Sheilah Graham was not generally known in 1941. Finally, he omitted Fitzgerald's note about writing a novel that would have to please both Scottie and Wilson.

The compositional method Fitzgerald employed for *The Last Tycoon* was his customary method of polishing his work through levels of revision. The first draft was always in holograph. Fitzgerald wrote in pencil on legal-size pads; he never worked on a typewriter. The holograph would be typed by a secretary—the typing for *The Last Tycoon* was done by Frances Kroll, his secretary in the 1939–40 period—usually with two carbon copies and sometimes with three. Fitzgerald would then heavily revise one or more of these typescripts, turning the one he preferred over to the typist for retyping. This process might continue through as many as four or five complete typescripts. Then he would revise again in proof.[1]

Some 1100 pages of drafts for the novel survive, including all typescripts and carbon copies. In addition, there are more than 200 pages of notes and related material.

In the inventory of drafts provided here, *manuscript* always means holograph. When a draft is typed, it is always called a *typescript*. Ribbon typescripts and carbon copies are differentiated. *Revised* means revised by Fitzgerald. Bracketed page numbers are inferential. Parenthetical paginations indicate Fitzgerald's own custom of replacing two or more pages with a single page: (30–31) indicates that he deleted pages 30 and 31 and replaced them with a page he numbered 30–31 for the benefit of the typist. A single bracket stands for "changed to." Thus #2 [v.3 means that Fitzgerald changed the draft designation from "2" to "v.3"—with "v." signifying "version." In the inventories that follow, the letters A, B, C, etc. are not Fitzgerald's; they have been supplied as a convenience for identifying draft stages or segments. The latest typescript for each episode is identified in the inventory, and it is always the copy-text used in Edmund Wilson's edition of *The Last Tycoon*.

In preparing Fitzgerald's typescripts for publication Wilson renumbered the pages and sometimes altered the episode headings. Wilson's handwriting can be differentiated from Fitzgerald's, but, it is not possible to identify the source of cross-outs.

In this study the manuscripts and typescripts are transcribed exactly. Passages or words Fitzgerald crossed out or deleted are enclosed in angle brackets. In a few cases where the deleted material is unrecoverable, empty angle brackets are used.

CHAPTER I

A   Manuscript. [1]–54 (54–55) 56–66 "Chapter I."

B   Revised Typescript & Manuscript. [1]–13 [14–15] 16–̈, [33–35]. "CHAPTER I." #1

C   Revised Carbon Copy. [1]–4 [ ] 5–25. With shorthand notes. "CHAPTER I." #1

D   Revised Typescript. [1]–8, insert 8, 9–10, 10½, 11–21, 21½, 22–24, 24, 25. "CHAPTER I." #2 [v.3

E   Carbon Copy. [1]–25. "CHAPTER I." #2

F   Typescript. [1]–17, 17A, 18–24. "CHAPTER I." #v.3

G   Carbon Copy. [1]–17, 17A, 18–24. "CHAPTER I." #v.3

Chapter I

Though I haven't ever been on the screen ~~there in fact~~, I was brought up in pictures. Rudolph ~~Valentino~~ came to my fifth birthday party, or so I was told — and I'm one of the few people who know how William Dean Taylor died. This, however, is a sort of trade secret and as it happened in 1922, ~~just~~ before my first Confession, it has no possible place in this last one. I mention it only to indicate that even before the age of reason, and whether I wanted to or not, I was in a position to watch the wheels go round.

I was going to write my memoirs once "The Producers Daughter", but at ~~eighteen~~ you never quite get around to

The opening of the novel: Chapter 1, Segment A.—F. Scott Fitzgerald Papers, Princeton University Library

H   Revised Carbon Copy. [1]–17, 17A, 18–19, 19½, 20–24, 24.
     "CHAPTER I." # v.3 [v.4
I   Revised Typescript. [1]–25. "CHAPTER I (Episodes 1, 2, 3)."
     #v.4 *Latest Typescript.*
     Variant opening: ("–It was still 'roses, roses all the way' down to
        1935—")
J   Manuscript. 4–6 [7]. "Chapter I"
K   Typescript. 5–7. "CHAPTER I." #1

Sanitarium Frame

L   Revised Typescript. [1]–3.   #3
M   Carbon Copy. [1]–3.   #3
N   Revised Typescript. [1]–3.   #4
O   Carbon Copy. [1]–3.   #4
P   Revised Typescript. [1]–4.   #5
Q   Typescript. [1]–3.   #6.
R   Carbon Copy. [1]–3   #6

Outline

A   1. The plane   June 28th
     2. Nashville
     3. Up forward. Different

On the basis of the surviving drafts, Chapter 1 (corresponding to
episodes 1–3) gave Fitzgerald little trouble. But the evidence is incomplete, for it is almost certain that there were discarded early
starts—see segments J and K. The first extant draft (A) for this
chapter consists of 66 holograph pages up to Stahr's conversation
with the pilot, breaking off with: " 'Look, you've got ect. see copy."
The material is complete up to that point—with no serious holes
and no important material that was subsequently cut. The inserted
typed page numbered (54–55) that describes Stahr's boyhood indicates that Fitzgerald probably had other early drafts that he con-

flated into this long holograph draft. Cecelia's last name here is
Bradogue, which Sheilah Graham informed Edmund Wilson was
changed because Fitzgerald decided it was too harsh-sounding.[2] He
changed it to *Baird* and then *Brady.* Wylie White was originally
named Rogers Carling. There is a problem in this first draft that
remains in the subsequent drafts: Cecelia does not recognize Mr.
Smith as Stahr when she first sees him on the plane. While it is
true that she sees only his back, she does hear his voice; and she
knows him very well. The obvious explanation is that Fitzgerald
wanted to delay introducing Stahr to the reader in order to develop
some curiosity about him; but the technique is a bit clumsy.

The Manny Schwartze material remained substantially un-
changed in the drafts of Chapter 1, indicating that Fitzgerald was
apparently satisfied with it. Nevertheless, Schwartze's function in
the novel is not clear. At one point Fitzgerald seems to have
planned for Schwartze to tell Stahr something that Stahr uses
against Brady in the unwritten blackmail episodes, since the memo
on the roadhouse raid has Fitzgerald's holograph note "For Schwartze." The main problem with the Schwartze material is that it
introduces Stahr as a callous figure—which he is not. Schwartze
commits suicide after Stahr rebuffs him, leaving a note for Stahr
saying that he knows it is no use if Stahr has turned against him.
While the suicide conveys a sense of the respect in which Stahr is
held, it is difficult to justify in terms of the novel's action. The only
way in which Schwartze can be said to function in the plan of the
novel is that his attempt to warn Stahr of a plot against him prepares
the reader for the power struggle between Brady and Stahr, but this
information is not really required in Chapter 1. Perhaps Fitzgerald
was attracted by the symmetry of opening and closing the novel with
deaths: Schwartze commits suicide during a plane trip, and Stahr
will die in a plane crash. Sheilah Graham's 11 January 1941 letter
to Maxwell Perkins explains that Fitzgerald had decided to either
cut out Schwartze "or find some way of bringing him into the rest of
the book."

The 32-page ribbon typescript (B) prepared from the holograph
was designated draft 1 or version 1. It was heavily revised, and 4
holograph pages were inserted—pp. 27–28 and 31–32—for the stew-
ardess' report of Stahr's conversation with the pilot and the closing

description of the plane landing at Glendale. The report of Stahr's lecture to the pilot about decision-making, the analysis of Stahr's Daedalian qualities, and the description of the landing were supplied in this typescript. The presentation of Stahr as a man who has flown high to achieve an overview of life is one of the most delicate passages in the novel, a quintessential Fitzgerald passage in which he brilliantly suggests complex ideas. It is instructive to consider a discarded version of this passage.

When he came down out of the sky he saw the Glendale airport below him, bright as mischief, but awfully warm. The moon of California was straight ahead over the Pacific by the low lying lands of the Long Beach Naval Reserves. Further down, there was Huntington Park, and on the right, the great mutual blur of Santa Monica. Stahr loved these lights, each cluster. Stahr felt no apology for them. Stahr felt that he had made all this—or remade it—and all the clusters that he saw beneath him. All the clusters of lights were something he had arranged like a trouble-shooter on an electric job.

"This light here," he said, "I will make it brighter. This cluster here.

"And this I shall black-out, and this I will lay my hand on, reluctantly, cruelly, definitely, and squeeze and squeeze, and something dark, something I don't know—something I may have left behind me in the dark. But these lights, this brightness, these clusters of human hope, of wild desire—I shall take these lights in my fingers. I shall make them bright, and whether they shine or not, it is these fingers that they shall succeed or fail."

The great plane lowered, arched down a truncated sweep into the Glendale airport. It was always very exciting to get there.

Although the writing is superb, the tone is not right; Stahr seems megalomaniacal, and the point about his sense of humanity is not made.

This is the latest version:

[Segment I]

He had flown up very high to see, on strong wings when he was young. And while he was up there he had looked on all the kingdoms, with the kind of eyes that can stare straight into the sun. Beating his wings tenaciously—finally frantically—and keeping on beating them he had stayed up there longer than most of us, and then, remembering all he had seen from his great height of how things were, he had settled gradually to earth.

The motors were off and all our five senses began to readjust themselves for landing. I could see a line of lights for the Long Beach Naval Station ahead and to the left, and on the right a twinkling blur for Santa Monica. The California moon was out, huge and orange over the Pacific. However I happened to feel about these things—and they were home after all—I know that Stahr must have felt much more. These were the things I had first opened my eyes on, like the sheep on the back lot of the old Laemmle studio; but this was where Stahr had come to earth after that extraordinary illuminating flight where he saw which way we were going, and how we looked doing it, and how much of it mattered. You could say that this was where an accidental wind blew him but I don't think so. I would rather think that in a "long shot" he saw a new way of measuring our jerky hopes and graceful rogueries and awkward sorrows, and that he came here from choice to be with us to the end. Like the plane coming down into the Glendale airport, into the warm darkness.

Ribbon copy (B) was an expansion of itself—with new typed pages interpolated—because its carbon copy (C) is 25 pages. The carbon copy has revisions in another hand, as well as shorthand notes and shorthand inserts. In the early stages of work Fitzgerald tried to dictate revisions to his secretary, a method he had acquired at studio script conferences.

The next level of revision for Chapter 1 is the typescript draft designated 2, which survives in a heavily revised ribbon copy (D) and an untouched carbon copy (E). After Fitzgerald revised the ribbon copy, he altered the draft number from 2 to v.3—indicating that this second working typescript was to be retyped as version 3. Fitzgerald's revisions in the typescripts for Chapter 1 are all in the nature of stylistic polishing; there is no new action.

The third typescript draft exists in three copies: an unrevised ribbon copy (F), an unrevised carbon copy (G), and a revised carbon copy (H) which Fitzgerald indicated was to be retyped as v.4.

The fourth typescript draft survives in only a revised ribbon copy

(I). Although it is the latest draft, Fitzgerald did not regard it as the final draft. At the head of the first page he wrote: "Rewrite from mood. Has become stilted with rewriting Don't look rewrite from mood". The same note was made on the carbon copy (G) of the third typescript.

With the first chapter belongs a trial opening of four holograph pages (J) and three typed pages (K), describing the take-off from Newark airport and listing the passengers.

[Segment K]

CHAPTER I

—It was still "roses, roses all the way" down to 1935—for me anyhow. For I had enough good looks and more than that amount of youth, and there was abundant money. It was fun to be discreetly superior on the coast because I went to Smith College in Northhampton, Mass., and to be rather mysteriously awesome in the East because of father's potential ability to make anyone a picture star. Of course this was nonsense, and I never encouraged such an idea among my friends. But I've been enough around Jewish people—and Jewish people are continental whether they think so or not—to be a realist about such matters.

Anyhow it was mostly roses, roses—especially that June with exams over, getting on the Douglass Mainliner to fly back home. Father had written that everything was better and better and enclosed me a check for—but I won't make you hate me by saying how much. I had bought a regular trousseau for myself and gifts for everybody I liked except Stahr. It was kind of unimaginable getting anything for him. A little like buying a present for Santa Claus. Oh, I admit I looked all over Brooks Brothers for something but I simply couldn't do it in the end. Nothing was quite right. Don't laugh—or there won't be any more story.

The plane left Newark airport at 4:30 and by five we had all stuffed our chewing gum furtively into the little ash holders—and then there was nothing much except getting used to the motors and to the usual qualms, and finding out who was on board. I'd seen the list in the airport—Lee Spurgeon, Stoner, Mortimer, Fleishhacker,

Gratteciel—but these might be phoney names for people I knew. I just sat for awhile—hours I guess—and wondered if anybody was liable to come into my life on this trip. I'd never been *in* pictures but I was very much *of* them—and I had an actress psychology about staring straight ahead in any new situation—until I found where I was.

My father, James Bradogue, was a self-made man, half Irish and half Pennsylvania Dutch. He was a publicity man and then an agent and then an executive and then a capitalist like now. I was born about when the "Birth of a Nation" was previewed, I guess. I know Rudolph Valentino came to my fifth birthday party. I can remember when there wasn't any Garbo or Shearer and Crawford and I'm one of the few people who killed Desmond Taylor but you'll never find out about that from me. We were in the picture business just like other families are in the grain business or the furniture business and I just accepted it I guess, like an angel accepts heaven or a ghost accepts his haunted house. So except for a few odd stray moments—and most of them I'm going to tell you about—it never had any magic or romance or glamor for me.

The discarded opening narrative frame in which Cecelia is introduced as telling her story to fellow-patients at a desert tuberculosis sanitarium survives in six typescript and carbon drafts (L–Q), but there is no manuscript draft. The main problem with this frame is that it sets up a narrative within a narrative. In his early notes Fitzgerald refers to the "recorder"—that is, the person who is reporting Cecelia's narrative. Cecelia's story was being reported by one or two outsiders: "What follows is our imperfect version of her story." Fitzgerald abandoned this method, which is unnecessarily cumbersome—particularly since Cecelia has to document the parts of her story that she learned from other figures. Sheilah Graham thinks that Fitzgerald considered salvaging the sanitarium material as the conclusion for the novel.

[Segment P]

We two men were fascinated by that young face. A few months ago, we had made a short trip to the canyons of the Colorado as if for a last gape at life; now back at the hospital this girl's face in the sunset, and with the fever, seemed to share some of the primordial rose tints of that "natural wonder."

"Go on tell us," we said. "We don't know about such things."

She started to cough, changed her mind—as one can.

"I don't mind telling *you*. But why should our friends, the asthmas, have to hear?"

"They're going," we assured her.

We three waited, our heads leant back on our chairs, while a nurse marshalled a flustered little group that must have heard the remark—and edged them toward the sanitarium. The nurse cast a reproachful glance back at Cecelia as if she wanted to return and slap her—but the glance changed its mind and the nurse hurried in after her flock.

"They're gone. Now tell us."

Cecelia stared up at the brilliant Arizona sky. She regarded it—the blue air, which to us had once stood for hope in the morning—not with regret but rather with the cocksure confusion of those the depression caught in mid-adolescence. Now she was twenty-five.

"Anything you want to know," she promised. "I don't owe *them* any loyalty. Oh, they fly over and see me sometimes, but what do I care—I'm ruined."

"We're all ruined," I said mildly.

She sat up, the Atzec figures of her dress emerging from the Navajo pattern of her blanket. The dress was thin—gone native for the sun country—and I remembered the round shining knobs of another girl's shoulders at another time and place but here we must all stay in the shadow.

"You shouldn't talk like that," she assured me, "I'm ruined, but you're just two good guys who happened to get a bug."

"You don't grant us any history," we objected with senescent irony, "Nobody over forty is allowed a history."

"I didn't mean that. I mean you'll get *well*."

"In case we don't, tell us the story. You still hear this stuff about him. What was he: Christ in Industry? I know boys who worked on the coast and hated his guts. Were you crazy about him? Loosen up, Cecelia. Something for a jaded palette! Think of the hospital dinner we'll face an half an hour."

Cecelia's glance suspected, then rejected our existence—not our right to live but our right to any important feeling of loss or passion or hope or high excitement. She started to talk, waited for a tickle to subside in her throat.

"He never looked at me," she said indignantly, "And I won't talk about him when you're in this mood."

She threw off the blanket and stood up, her center-parted hair falling from her wan temples, ripples from a brown dam. She was high-breasted and emaciated, still perfectly the young woman of her time. Superiority was implicit in her heel taps as she walked through the open door into the corridor of the building—our only road to wonderland. Apparently Cecelia believed in nothing at present, but it seemed she had once know another road, passed by it a long time ago.

We were sure, nevertheless, that sometime she would tell us about it—and so she did. What follows is our imperfect version of her story.

CHAPTER II (*Episodes 4–6*)

A   Manuscript. [1–13]. "Chapter II."

B   Revised Carbon Copy & Revised Typescript. [26] 27–29, 29½ (30–31), 32–33 [inserts A & B] 34–36, 36½, 36½A, 37–39. "CHAPTER II." #2

C   Typescript. [26] 27–29, 31–38. "CHAPTER II." #2 #1

D   Revised Carbon Copy. [33]–34. #2

E   Manuscript & Revised Carbon Copy. [1] 1½, 2, 2½, 3, 3½. "Chapter II." #v.2

F   Revised Typescript & Manuscript. [1] 2–9. "CHAPTER II." #2

G   Revised Typescript. 25–31. "CHAPTER II." #v.2

H   Manuscript & Revised Typescript. 1–5. "Chapter II." #2 [#3.]

I   Revised Typescript. [25] 26–29. "CHAPTER II." #3

J   Manuscript & Revised Typescript. 1–7 [8–18].

K   Revised Typescript. 30–33. #3

L   Revised Carbon Copy. [26] 27–33, "CHAPTER II." #2

M   Revised Typescript. 1–4, 6, 5, 6, 7–9. "CHAPTER II." #4/#v. 1

N   Carbon Copy. [25]–30. "CHAPTER II." #4. 3 copies

O   Revised Carbon Copy. 29–36, [insert], 37–38

P   Carbon Copy. [1–4].

Q   Manuscript. g–k.

R   Manuscript. 1–12.

S   Typescript. 20, 33–36, [37]

T   Manuscript. [1–17]. "Chap II (Part III)."

U   Typescript. 1–5

V   Revised Carbon Copy. 43

W   Manuscript. 1–20. "Episodes 4 and Five"; "Episode 6 (7 is out)." *Latest Holograph.*

X   Revised Carbon Copy. 1–6. "Episodes 4 and 5."

Y   Revised Typescript. 1–6. "Episodes 4 and 5." *Latest Typescript.*

Z   Carbon Copy. 1–3. "Episode 6."

AA   Revised Typescript. 1–3. "Episode 6." *Latest Typescript.*

Outline

B   4. Johnny Swanson—Marcus leaving—Brady   July 28th

      5. The Earthquake

      6. The Back lot

    The earliest holograph draft for the opening of Chapter 2 (episodes 4–6) appears to be thirteen fragmentary unnumbered pages (A) describing the studio at night and the earthquake. In this material Cecelia addresses an aside to "my gallant gentlemen," indicating that at this point Fitzgerald still intended to use the sanitarium frame. The account of Stahr's first sight of Thalia (Kathleen) is missing, but after Stahr falls into a pool of water Cecelia reports that

"She came up to him, right like a tart, I suppose and wiped him off." Although Cecelia does justice to Thalia's beauty, her application of terms like "tart" and "trollop" to Thalia may indicate that Fitzgerald was preparing the reader for the information that Thalia has had an active sexual history. Or perhaps these terms were only meant to convey Cecelia's resentment of Thalia.

Thalia was the muse of comedy and bucolic poetry. Sheilah Graham reports in *The Real F. Scott Fitzgerald* (p. 180) that Fitzgerald changed the name from *Thalia* to *Kathleen* after she told him about a London showgirl named Thalia who burned to death when her hair caught fire. The character is not named in the later drafts for this chapter.

At least one layer of draft for this section of the novel has been lost, for there is no complete first typescript. The earliest surviving typescript is an incomplete fifteen-page draft (B) assembled from ribbon copy pages of one typescript and carbon pages from another typescript. It is heavily revised by Fitzgerald and also in shorthand. Three of the pages are designated "2"—indicating that this draft conflates two levels of typescript. The unrevised ribbon copy (C) numbered [26]–38 was partly copied from the conflated draft (B) and is itself a conflation; it is identified on seven pages as "2," but the last two pages are marked "1"—indicating that these pages were salvaged from the missing first typescript. Ribbon copy (C) forms a complete episode—except for missing p. 30—up to Stahr's encounter with Thalia. In this typescript Robinson introduces Stahr to his ne'er-do-well brother, Horace, who is in some kind of unspecified trouble and needs a job. Almost certainly Fitzgerald was planting Horace Robinson for later use in the novel, a plan which was soon abandoned. Since both of these drafts begin at page number 26 work on them followed completion of the 25–page latest typescript for Chapter 1. At this early stage of composition Fitzgerald was still trying to finish and polish one chapter at a time—instead of drafting the whole novel—in order to have 15,000 words of material to show *Collier's*.

Stahr's first name is given as "Munroe" in these early drafts; but it is uncertain if a simple spelling problem was involved. Fitzgerald's notes indicate that he originally considered giving Stahr the first name "Irving"—which would have made the identification with Irving Thalberg too strong. Fitzgerald then tried the name "Milton" before settling on Monroe. The name "Stahr" requires no explication, but it is perhaps worth noting that the slogan of MGM in the thirties was "More Stars Than There Are in Heaven."

There is a two-page carbon copy (D) describing Thalia at the moment Stahr helps rescue her in the flood, marked "OLD CHAP II (Restaurant Scene"—perhaps an indication that Fitzgerald planned to use it elsewhere in the novel.

[Segment D]

⟨it was hard to say.⟩ She looked, for a split second, like an out-and-out adventuress ⟨—the sort of girl that boys see in the front row of the chorus once when they are young—and who afterwards subconsciously influences their entire love life. As I say, she was that way, for a split second—⟩ as "common" as they come, ready for anything male—a wench, a free booter, an outsider.

And then Stahr saw that she was a raving beauty, ⟨hapless and helpless at the moment, no doubt, but even so, giving the impression of living half way between heaven and earth—infinitely piteous.⟩ Something about her made one catch one's breath, choke back any last thought of ⟨your⟩ ones own self, ⟨your own well being—and "knocked your eye out," as they say.

Not the professional kind of beauty either. I could forgive that in retrospect.⟩ She was not the kind that chokes up the areas of dinner parties in our little town on the coast giving no other woman breathing room, but rather like Constance Talmadge was once—from all reports. I can't confirm the reports, because all I remember about Constance when I was a little girl was just her laughter, and then her being ready to laugh, and then *bang!* more laughter.

Perhaps that's beauty—perhaps that's what Stahr saw in his Thalia then: laughter, and then doubt as to whether it was time to laugh, and then, always waiting around the corner—more laughter.

I hate to intrude myself into the picture, even for contrast, but *I'm* not like that. I wait till I'm amused. Even if I'm trying to please someone. But Thalia was *all* laughter. Her face just set that way. Even if she said nothing more important than "What! Darling?" with her eyes all tinkling at the edges.

it was hard to say. She looked, for a split second, like ~~an out~~ *her*

brazen image that

~~and-out adventuress--the sort of girl that~~ boys ~~see in~~ the front *pick out of*

row of the chorus once when they are young--and who afterwards *possibly*

~~subconsciously~~ influence ~~their entire love life.~~ As I say, she *The mirror of their souls. For that second*

~~was that way, for a split second~~ *shows* --as "common" as they come, ready

for anything ~~make~~--a wench, a free-booter, an outsider.

And then Stahr saw that she was a ~~living~~ beauty, hapless *great*

~~and helpless~~ at the moment, ~~no doubt,~~ but even~~, so, giving the~~ *now as she smiled around*

~~impression of~~ living half way between heaven and earth~~. Individually~~ *her wet clothes, giving*

~~piteous. Something about her made one catch one's breath,~~ choke *Once if*
It means more, she

~~back any last thought of your own self, your own well being--and~~

"knocked your eye out", as they say.

Not the professional kind of beauty either. I could *have*

forgive~~N~~ that, in retrospect. She was not the kind that chokes up *because in the long run professional beauties are in-*

the areas of dinner parties ~~in our little town on the coast giving~~ *effectual — they clog up* *and do all the breathing for*

~~no other woman breathing room, but rather like Constance Talmadge~~ *everybody, so finally even the men half a go outside for air. Ho-*

~~was one--from all reports. I can't confirm the reports, because~~ *Thalia's weapon was laughter, first, being not ready to*

~~all I remember about Constance when I was a little girl was just~~ *laugh at all times and then — never disappointing you*

~~her laughter, and then her being ready to laugh, and then bang!~~

~~more laughter.~~

when it came. Perhaps that's beauty--perhaps that's what Stahr saw in

his Thalia then: laughter ~~and then doubt as to whether~~ it was time *waiting around the corner, and then —*
an everlasting reservoir of more

~~to laugh, and then, always waiting around the corner~~--more laughter. *laughter.*

I hate to intrude myself into the picture, even for con-

trast, but I'm not like that. I wait till I'm amused, ~~even~~ if I'm *even*

trying to please someone. But Thalia was ~~all laughter. Her face~~ *S*

just set that way, ~~even if she said nothing more important than~~

~~"Darling."~~ with her eyes all ~~tinkling~~ at the edges. *from* *twinkling* *Its the beautiful* *small teeth with the flash*

~~You were chocked at her beauty. Let me admit that and~~

~~get it over with. It was enough to keep one awake at night.~~ *of gleaming red above them. It was all a*

⟨You were shocked at her beauty. Let me admit that and get it over with. It was enough to keep one awake at night.⟩

It was there too when she moved. Everybody has had the excitement of seeing an apparent beauty from afar; and then, after a moment, as that same face grew mobile—watching the beauty disappear second by second, as if a lovely statue had begun to walk with the meager joints of a paper doll. There was nothing of that in Thalia.

She came right up to him, took his handkerchief out of his breast-pocket and wiped off his hands, with that laughter, I suppose.

⟨I can hear it now! Thinking of it makes me remember the time when I lost my boy. When he played the piano over and over to that girl Reina, and I realized at last that I wasn't wanted. That piano in a little New England roadhouse near Smith, playing Jerome Kern over and over. The keys falling like leaves; his hands and then her hands over them splayed as she showed him a black chord. I was a freshman then.⟩

Another holograph chapter opening of six pages (with one page of carbon) is designated "v2" on the first page (E). It goes up to Stahr's departure from his office for the flood site and introduces Robinson. There is no typescript for this material.

The next stage of the opening of Chapter 2 is nine pages of ribbon copy, carbon copy, and holograph marked "V.2" (F). Here Robinson asks Stahr to hire his brother, and the women are rescued from the head of Vishnu. Stahr is struck by the beauty of one of the women, but the encounter is not developed. The segment ends with Stahr leaving to change his wet clothes. Related to this segment is a seven-page ribbon typescript (G) marked "2" that Fitzgerald stripped: "Stet whats marked only. Destroy the rest." It is longer than segment (F) and closes with an analysis of Stahr's prestige with his employees and a description of his office.

The change from Vishnu to Siva for the prop from which Kathleen is rescued indicates the pains Fitzgerald took with minor details. Vishnu is the Hindu god regarded by Vishnavas as the supreme diety. Siva is the Hindu diety representing the principle of destruction as well as the reproductive or restoring power; Siva is also the great ascetic, the worker of miracles. It is appropriate for

Stahr and Kathleen to be brought together through the agency of Siva, for Kathleen embodies the elements of both Stahr's restoration to life and his destruction.

The earliest identifiable segment of the next draft is a five-page holograph and revised ribbon copy description of the studio at night, the earthquake, and the rescue of the women (H). The two pages of typescript in (H) were originally marked "2" but changed to "3." This opening sequence was retyped and revised as "3" (I). By now Horace Robinson had been removed.

The third-draft typescript opening is continued by eighteen pages of holograph and revised ribbon copy (J). Here the first encounter between Stahr and Thalia is expanded by his insistence on getting her dry clothing. He takes her to the wardrobe department and talks about his work: "But when you grow older you'll find that anywhere anything much goes on it is always very quiet." Stahr returns to his office and phones Cecelia, who provides two versions of the call—one in which Stahr asks her to have a cup of tea with him, and another in which Thalia was apparently in Stahr's office ("Of course I had no idea who was there."). Related to draft (J) are a four-page revised typescript (K) of Stahr's conversation with Thalia, and a revised carbon copy of the opening of the chapter (L).

The fourth typescript draft survives in two forms: a ten-page revised ribbon copy (M) salvaged from "v. 1" with two pages marked "4," and three copies of unrevised carbons (N) of a different version "4." These versions differ in their treatment of Stahr's first meeting with Thalia. In (M) Stahr notices that one of the women is beautiful, but she makes no great impression on him. In (N) Cecelia analyzes Thalia's effect on Stahr and describes her laugh.

There are also discarded scenes for Chapter 2. Revised carbon copy (O) with shorthand notes describes the flood and the meeting between Stahr and Thalia, in which she wipes him off. A four-page carbon copy (P) has Stahr escorting the rescued women to their car and then returning to his office.

The interesting holograph paged g–k (Q) reports the conversation between Stahr and Thalia in the commissary, where he takes her after helping to rescue her. Thalia checks the soaked contents of her purse and discovers that her tickets for a track meet have been lost, which triggers Stahl's thoughts about his boyhood:

[Segment Q]

It wasn't his old talking when he said Ill make it up to you. He wasn't sorry for her because he had no use for all he had or what he was offered. As far as amusement, he had been happier in New York when he was a kid at the knowledge that he could get into Wendts bowling joint every Thursday or could bet on Friday at Skorksi's and if he won watch the big boys in the evening.

It was just a horrible sense of waste as he thought of all the stuff that came to him now and how little he could do to it, not even pass it out or find anyone who wanted it now a days. And this girl's two paste boards had floated out into a sea of mud, maybe meaning all to her against an empty afternoon as it had meant to his mother that day when she had lost the tickets for the Menorah festival. It must have been that for he would always rather do things than watch other people do them. But he knew what defeated anticipation meant in human life so he said,

"Look tomorrow I'm going ect.

Except for a brief description of Stahr as a gang leader in the Bronx, nothing is provided about Stahr's boyhood in the latest drafts of the novel. The revisions in Chapter 2 are in the direction of compactness or foreshortening. It is sufficient for Stahr to be shown functioning at the peak of his ability; background on his boyhood does not necessarily add to the characterization. For his own use, however, Fitzgerald wrote a background sketch about Stahr—in which he obviously used the facts of Thalberg's career. Fitzgerald needed to know all about his hero, but it was not obligatory for the reader to have the information. (See Sheilah Graham's 11 January 1941 letter to Maxwell Perkins in Chapter 6 below.)

Stahr will have to be born in New York or Brooklyn or Newark. Remember the story in which Carl Laemele kept making long distance calls asking about this and that fact and getting answers from a voice who described himself vagule as the assistant and describing troubles that he had had with perforationss in certain films that had been faulty and how he had to go to Selig in Philadelphia and give him the right to make the prints in order to get him to correct the faulty perforation in the films caused by an imperfect jointure of the work of several cameras. Look up that incident in "A million and one nights."

Also this assistant had settled several difficult negotiations with stage actors and actresses who were wanted on the coast. Though the assistant described various of these endeavors to the Eastern manager, who had really been sick or on a bust or occupied in some affairs of his own during this time; Laemele after a month became rather puzzled about the situation and said very much as follows:

"Say, I have been spending anywhere from twenty to a hundred dollars on thse calls and there have been plenty of them and I never manage to find that fellow in. He must be awfully busy running around and, by the way, who are you? You say you're an assistant. Who are you?"

Whereupon Stahr answers:

"Well, to tell you the truth, Mr. Laemele, I'm the office boy."

Whereupon, Laemele swore and when he calmed down a little, he said: "No you're not, you're not the office boy, you're the Eastern Manager."

Fitzgerald's early biographical sketch for Thalia shows that he originally conceived her as having a much less glamorous background than he invented for Kathleen, although Thalia's domestic situation was extremely complex:

THALIA was born in 1908 in Newfoundland.

She was married in '29 to a rich man who came to Newfoundland as a tourist and loved her. She came of very humble parents. father was captain of a fishing snack and it was a run-away marriage. She married this wealthy man who had a place there. They had an awful time about their marriage because he was married. She had to live with him a year before he could divorce his wife and marry her.

One of the children of the first marriage died. It was blamed on her because if the divorce had not occurred and she hadn't appeared, it would not have happened. Her husband went all to pieces, lost all his money and she is still taking care of him in a vague way and he is perhaps in a sanitarium in the East and perhaps dead.

She came to California as a companion of the wife (KIKI) who is divorced and who leans on her altogether and at times is very grateful to her and sometimes turns on her for breaking up her home. She has become a great friend of this wife—both of whom love this man—and has stepped in and helped by giving up her own plans and what money there was. The wife is kind of a broken neurotic who has dabbled in dope and Thalia is haunted by the idea that she has broken up this home and doesn't know what her position is—she did it for love, etc., but she did break up this home, she feels.

The first wife has a little girl left from the marriage. She takes care of this woman part of the time and also does part time work in her mornings, but has never considered the studios and when she meets Stahr it is absolutely unimportunate.

Her position in the home has gradually drifted into that of an upper servant because she unfortunately was too generous in a moment of feeling of atonement. She has been having an affair intermittant of which she is half ashamed, with the character whom I have called Robinson the cutter who is in his: (and this is very important) professional life an extraordinarily interesting and subtle character on the idea of Sergeant Johnson in the army or that cutter at United Artists whom I so admired or any other person of the type of trouble shooter or film technician—and I want to contrast this sharply with his utter conventionality and acceptance of banalities in the face of what might be called the cultural urban world. Women can twist him around their little finger. He might be able to unravel the most twisted skein of wires in a blinding snowstorm on top of a sixty foot telephone pole in the dark with no more tools than an imperfect pair of pliers made out of the nails of his boots. but faced with the situation which the most ignorant and useless person would handle with urbanity he would seem helpless and gauky—so much so as to give the impression of being a Babbitt or of being a stupid, gawky, inept fellow.

This contrast at some point in the story is recognized by Stahr who must at all points, when possible, be pointed up as a man who sees below the surface into reality.

Her attitude towards this man has been that even in the niceties of love-making she has had to be his master and his deep gratitude to her is allied to his love for her though throughout the story he always feels that she is inevitably the superior person. Stahr at some point points it out to her that this is nonsense and I want to show here something different in mens' and women's points of view: particularly that women are prone to cling to an advantage or rather have less human generosity in points of character than men have, or do I mean a less wide point of view?

Thalia's relationship with Robinson was to have motivated him to join Brady's conspiracy against Stahr in the original plot of the novel. At one stage Fitzgerald considered that Robinson would be the man selected to murder Stahr or that Stahr would plan Robinson's murder:

> The man chosen tentatively to put Stahr out of the way is Robinson the cutter. Must develop Robinson character so that this is possible, that is Robinson now has 3 aspects. His top possibility as a sort of Sergeant Johnson character as planned. His relation with the world which is conventional and rather stereotyped and trite and this new element in which it would be possible for him to be so corrupted by circumstance as to be drawn into such a matter and used by Bradogue. To do this it is practically necessary that there must be from the beginning some flaw in Robinson in spite of his courage, his resourcefulness, his technical expertness and the Sergeant Johnson virtues I intend to give him. Some secret flaw—perhaps something sexual. It might be possible, but if I do that, then he could have had no relation with Thalia who certainly would not have accepted a bad lover. Perhaps he would have some flaw, not sexual—not unmanly—in any case have no special idea at present, and this must be invented. In any case, his having loved Thalia would make him a very natural tool for Bradogue to use in playing on his natural jealousy of Stahr.

Compactness or dramatic impact also dictated Fitzgerald's decision to hone Stahr's first encounter with Thalia to a glimpse. In the latest draft it is literally love at first sight for Stahr, although his reaction is delayed.

Chapter 2 underwent a steady process of reduction through the draft stages as Fitzgerald sharpened the focus and cut out expository action. Two linked scenes at the end of the chapter were delted: the twelve-page holograph quarrel between Wylie White and Stahr (R), and the seventeen-page holograph section in which Stahr hears Brady plotting against him (T)—both of which also survive in type-scripts (S and U) separated from the working drafts.

[Segment S]

His night secretary stood in a listening attitude in front of the closed door of the main office.

"There's someone inside, Mr. Stahr," she said in alarm, "I went to the wash-room and when I came back someone had gotten in and locked the door from the inside. I didn't know quite what to do—I think from his voice it's Mr. White."

Stahr tried the door.

"Wylie?" he called.

After a moment a blurred voice answered him.

"Just second. I'm engaged on the phone."

"Let me in, you dope!" Stahr ordered impatiently. The receiver clicked and Wylie came to the door. He was deeply, vitally drunk.

"I've been putting in calls," he said, "—in your name."

"Who to?" demanded Stahr.

"Everybody—The department of Forestry in Washington, the newspapers, the commissary—I ordered you twisted fish and a cat's handle-bar and they keep calling back about it. And I called the Navy in San Diego and ordered a cruiser to take you down the Mississippi—to spot locations for Tom Sawyer. I told the publicity department all our stars were killed in the earthquake and I told 'em to play it up *big*—"

Stahr opened the door and spoke briefly to the secretary.

"Trace Mr. White's calls on my private wire and see what he's done and fix it up."

He closed the door sharply, went over to White and smashed him in the face. Wylie staggered against the table. He outweighed Stahr by forty pounds and presently he got his balance and took a step forward.

"You God damned drunk," cried Stahr. "I told you to stay sober. Get off this lot and if I ever see you again I'll ruin you."

Wylie White's hand fell heavily on Stahr's shoulder. Stahr shook it off and hit him again in the face.

"I'm through with you," he raged, "I pulled you through D.T.'s and gave you another chance—"

Wylie's arm tensed to throw a punch that would have floored Stahr but the second blow or the words that went with it seemed to sober him. He sat down on a great couch sinking his face in his hands.

"Get out!" cried Stahr, his hand fumbling on his desk for something to hurl. Then suddenly his temper broke too, and he said "Hell's bells," and sat down behind his desk looking at his bleeding knuckles.

"What was the idea?" he demanded. A sudden kindliness, a quick ray as spontaneous as his outbreak, came into his face. The short flash of a smile showed forgiveness, shame, affection.

"Oh, I just got tired hearing what a great man you are, Monroe," said Wylie coldly, "Somebody told me once too often. Because they're wrong. Two years ago most of the boys around here would have died for you, but times have changed and you don't read the signs. You're doing a costume part and you don't know it—the brilliant capitalist of the twenties. But these secretaries and typists that have been living on hay since '29—they don't see themselves as Joan Crawford characters anymore. They want to eat."

Stahr was silent—it was as good a time as any to pump Wylie.

"You can suppress them easy enough or replace them but you better keep you hands off the writers."

"You promised me you were through with politics," Stahr reminded him. He took a suit from a wardrobe closet, and began to shed his wet clothes.

"If you'd give me a producer contract I'd be out of it," said Wylie. "As a writer I've got to be on one side or another—⟨and⟩ I can't be a god damn fink."

"I told you that when you'd been sober two years I'd let you produce."

"Out here two years is a lifetime."

"Tonight isn't going to help," said Stahr, "And I'll be damned if you can come up here and blame me for the whole American system. I've fought Bradogue and his bastards till we're just about speaking and that's all. I've threatened to quit so often that I laugh when I say it. And now you boys turn on me. Why, I made you. Most of you are

once-a-week writers that couldn't earn a good living in the east—
maybe thirty a week on a newspaper. And we pay you enough for
chauffeurs and swimming pools.''

He was tieing his tie in the mirror.

"—and you kid yourself into thinking you're horny handed work-
ers. Some little tit still wet behind the ears called me a fascist the
other day.''

"You're done, Monroe," said Wylie stubbornly, "I like you because I'm a romantic but the times have passed you by. You don't
know what's happening.''

"When I was sixteen, Wylie, during the war, I was an office
monkey on the New York Call. I was there during the suppression
and the raids and all us boys read the Communist Manifesto and
swore by it.''

"I guess it didn't sink in.''

"In a way—but I'm not one of these natural believers always asking where the church is. Or the cathouse or the saloon either. Thinking's a lot harder than believing but it's more fun too. And it occurred to me that I was a better man than most of those fellows. If
they'd been planning to make me a big shot I might have played
along, but there wasn't any future.''

"That was a bad guess, Monroe.''

"Don't be so sure. I saw this world was going to function a little
longer anyhow. I couldn't breath with those people—nine-tenths of
them ready to sell out for a nickle. More dirty politics than there is in
a studio, and all covered up with holy talk, and not a laugh in a
carload. I became a Jew again. I swear I did. And I was a good one till
Minna died. A perfectly happy good Jew.''

⟨There was a silence for a moment as they both glanced at her
picture on his desk.

"I met a girl who reminded me of her tonight," said Stahr.

"Did you—where?''

"Out on the back lot. Do you remember how Minna smiled—as
if she was just ready for laughter—'' He broke off. "This woman
wanted to laugh tonight—in just the same way—and would have if
I'd looked at her and it would have been just like Minna. So I
didn't.''⟩

Wylie took advantage of this self-absorption to ask.

"Say have you got a drink?"

"Yes, but not for you. Your eyes are only just beginning to look human. I want to know why you're beginning to talk like a Red again. You're drifting back."

"No I'm not," said Wylie, "They wouldn't take me. I'm on the blacklist. They only want to use me."

"You going to let them?"

"Why not? I've got a conscience, Monroe. I was born a Catholic and a Catholic conscience takes a long time to kill. I couldn't fight them, I couldn't come out against them. They're pretty awful but they're right. You can make your smart speeches about how lousy they are and not one out of ten is anything but a holy Joe or a poor kid gone sour. But when you finished it's *you* who have to say 'So what?' to yourself."

"I don't say 'So what?' to myself," said Stahr sharply, "I told you in the plane coming out here that you were soft stuff—all of you. A bunch of soft mush letting yourselves be pushed around by boys that are going to get something out of it."

"Sure—I know. They'd liquidate us first of all. But I can't change myself—I've tried and I can't. My heart *and* my good sense, are with the—the dispossessed. If they eat me up then I'm just the husband of a black widow spider. That's my hard luck."

Stahr's mind was not on Wylie's immediate words. He needed a man, an intellectual, someone of force, heart, liberal opinions and popularity to split the movement among the writers. He had counted until this moment on Wylie White and now he was full of doubt both as to White's stability in the matter of drink and as to whether money was the coin to buy him with. So long as Wylie went on bats that was sufficient grounds for not making him a producer—though in fact Stahr kept his assistant producers close under his eyes so that they more nearly fulfilled the functions of supervisors, their former and less impressive title. But it was as a writer that he could best use Wylie.

The dictograph buzzed at his elbow; he switched it on.

"Mr. Stahr, are you taking calls?"

"Who is it?"

"Well, there's half a dozen. Joe Robinson left word that everything's all right And then Mr. Bradogue."

"I'll get him on the inter-office."
He pressed another button.

I was still on the couch in father's office. The doctor had been up to take a stitch in my hand—I was the only victim on the lot—and the drug he gave me made me doze for an hour. Father was in and out; he happened to be out when Stahr called.

"Come on over here and take charge of your friend, Wylie," Stahr said, "You can keep him out of the Clover Club and the clip-joints. He's on a college boy bust."

I did not know that at this point Wylie White got up quickly and said: "I'm going, Monroe. I don't want her to see me with this eye—you did it, you bastard. It's turning blue."

I saw Wylie though—from a distance out in the hall, though he didn't know it. I was excited about going to see Stahr but I suspected it would be highly impersonal.

"Wylie's gone," he said, "There was something the matter with his face and he didn't want you to see it. What

[Segment U]

That would have been all if I hadn't picked up the phone to call father. Then it transpired that the water mains had not suffered the only damage that night—for instead of talking to father I was suddenly listening to a conversation between him and someone on his private wire to New York.

". . . the whole back lot is a shambles," father's voice said, "My daughter was almost killed . . ."

I laughed and signalled to Stahr who picked up an extension and listened in with me.

". . . No, she's fine now. She went home by herself," said father. "The situation is the same. We can't do with him and we can't do without him."

"Why can't you?" said the voice. "If you can't find a competent executive out there we've got young men in our office that could learn the set-up in six months."

"We can find business men," said my father, "—too many. And

we can find production men. But business men who can make pictures don't grow on trees."

I looked at Stahr somewhat aghast. His shoulders were shaking in his effort not to laugh aloud.

"I don't know what to think, Billy," said the voice, "One month we hear he's a wonder man and the next month that he's an extravagant idealist. This isn't 1927. Money's hard to come by and if we're letting millions slip away on these masterpieces he's no man for us."

"I watch him like a cat," father said, "Whatever I don't like I throw in a monkey wrench." He paused, "Anyhow I don't think we have to worry for so long. I'm in touch with his doctor and he's shot to pieces. Let him work himself sick, then ship him off on a world cruise. We can still use him—his name will still mean a lot. It gets more work out of people if they think they're doing it for him."

For a minute I had been holding the receiver away from me like a snake's head. Now I hung up. Stahr was still listening but the smile was gone. After a moment he hung up too, and taking a ring off his finger, exactly like the one he had given me, began playing with it.

"Celia," he said thoughtfully, "When I meet Jew-haters I wonder if they feel about us like I do about the Irish."

I looked at him rather fearfully, I guess. I was rather glad at being only half Irish.

"Your father knows who built this studio out of nothing; he knows I could take over any studio in Hollywood tomorrow and this would be just a gutted factory. But treachery is something he loves more than money. He's more devious than any Jew out here. Maybe that's why they like him in Wall Street."

"Are you really sick?" I asked.

"Of course not," he said scornfully.

"Father's a pretty mean man," I said, after a minute, "I've never been able to love him—even as a little girl."

"Oh, you oughtn't to say that." He was a little shocked, "He's your father."

"He's your partner, and you certainly must loathe him."

"I don't loathe him," he assured me, almost with surprise, "You don't hate a man you can see through like glass. All that talk about throwing monkey-wrenches! He's never wrecked a single plan I cared about—sometimes I send him dead horses to kill. Why if he got out I'd miss him—in the grapevine he takes the raps for half my mistakes. If something goes wrong they say that's Billy Bradogue interfering with Monroe. That's the advantage of a reputation, Celia—the truth is I make most of the mistakes around here—but I'm a man who's easier to believe in."

He was smiling again.

"You're a good man, Monroe."

"Oh no," he said, "I'm too smart to get into mischief and I'm interested in people—I've collected a lot of them and try to take care of the good ones. But there's no such thing as a good man in big business."

He put his ring back in place and got up.

"Don't think this disturbed me. Two years ago Billy put a wire in my office downstairs and when I found he knew some things he oughtn't to know I got Joe Robinson on the trail. Then I tapped Billy's wires and we had some fun but it took too much time so I told him about it."

He looked at me closely.

"Just forget that about my health, will you, Celia—my doctor's a rat."

We went out together. It was long after midnight and the whole place seemed deserted except for two or three chauffeurs down by the commissary. I had never before heard my father speak of Stahr without respect and admiration and now I hated him for his wish that Stahr would die. Father liked to tell the story about when Stahr was an office boy in the New York offices of Films Par Excellence. Old Menges had come out to set up a West coast unit, leaving a general manager and one of the vice-presidents in charge in the East. He was getting regular communications from the manager and things were apparently going all right. Then he discovered that the Vice President had been in Florida three months and he telephoned the general manager. The first thing he heard was that the general manager had been taken sick the day he left.

"Well, who've I been communicating with?" he asked, "Who's been signing the letters? Who's been running things? Who is this I'm talking to now?"

"This is your office boy, Mr. Menges, this is Monroe Stahr."

Father's story was that Menges made him general manager on the spot. Anyhow he was out here at twenty-one running the old combine lot. Three years later he was already the "production genius" and Hollywood hero number one, though nobody out of California knew his name.

As we walked toward the new commissary I thought of some questions I wanted to ask Stahr. I was taking sociology that year.

"What are the general working conditions in the studio?" I asked, pretentiously.

"About average," he said rather surprised, "We don't run a sweat shop but we haven't got around to employees swimming pools."

"Wylie White says the writers work in little cubicles."

He laughed.

"The poor horny-handed writers," he said, Starving for sunshine and air. Well, most of the playwrights from the East work at home. The smart boys get to be producers or directors and have a suite. The others don't work too hard unless they're in conference in some producer's office. They're not really writers—they're well paid secretaries."

"They'd like that."

"Well, it's true. They're like children. You can't trust them so I have one work behind another on an idea—sometimes half a dozen working on the same script and not knowing about the others."

"You rate them low."

He nodded absently.

"Not when they write books or plays. But out here—"

He was putting me into my car and suddenly he clutched the doorhandle and fainted dead away on the pavement outside the commissary. Some chauffeurs rushed up, we threw water in his face and got him sitting up. In a minute he was all right again and concerned with how many people had seen him go down. He took father's chauffeur aside and spoke to him quickly, then he got in his own car. He wouldn't even let me ride home with home.

I knew then that he was probably going to die and I felt terribly sorry.

A single page of revised carbon copy (T) describes Thalia. At this point in the ontogeny of Chapter 2 Fitzgerald wrote a fresh twenty-page holograph draft (W) for episodes 4, 5, and 6—noting that "7 is out." But Fitzgerald did not head this material as Chapter 2, for at this stage he had shifted to the procedure of working his way through the episodes of his outline. The deleted episode 7 cannot be identified with certainty, but it was probably the telephone episode(s) printed above. Although it is a strong scene and prepares for the power struggle between Stahr and Brady, Fitzgerald may have felt that it tells too much too early by informing the reader that Stahr is a dying man. Holograph draft (W) became the latest version. It closes with a heroic view of Stahr, comparing him to Napoleon. Before writing the novel Fitzgerald read Froude's *Caesar*.

Segment (W) was typed in two parts: episodes 4 and 5 (six pages) and episode 6 (three pages). Both the ribbon copy (Y) and the carbon copy (X) for episodes 4 and 5 were revised, with the ribbon serving as the latest draft. The three-page ribbon copy (AA) for episode 6 was revised, but the carbon copy (Z) was not.

In rewriting Chapter 2 Fitzgerald reduced its size by half—removing Horace Robinson, trimming the first encounter between Stahr and Thalia to a glimpse, and cutting out all the post-flood material between Stahr and Cecelia. The purpose of this process was to condense an expository chapter into a tight, dramatic chapter.

EPISODE 7

A   Manuscript. [1]–12. "Episode 8"
B   Revised Carbon Copy. 1–6. "Episode 8 [7"
C   Revised Typescript. 1–5. "Episode 8 [7" *Latest Typescript*

Outline

C 7. The Camera man.   July 29th
     Stahr's work and health. From something she wrote.

Beginning with episode 7 (the opening of Wilson's Chapter 3), Fitzgerald worked rapidly, with little rewriting. It is clear that he had decided to finish a working draft of the whole novel—which he would then revise and restructure. There were at least two reasons for the change in procedure: Fitzgerald needed a complete draft in order to negotiate an advance from Scribners; and he had more plot than he could really accomodate in the projected 50,000-word limit; so he was proportioning the episodes by writing them.

Episode 7 was originally marked episode 8, but is redesignated 7 on the typescript and corresponds to the note for episode 7 in Fitzgerald's outline, as Cecelia describes Stahr's working day, assembling the data from several sources. Fitzgerald prepared a log of Stahr's day as a guide for describing it, but some of the material in the log does not appear in Fitzgerald's account.

C–D

(Stahr's Day)

Stahr and	)	KEEP FOR
News about Back lot	) 7	TIME SCHEDULE
Morgan's Fly	)	

11–11.30	*Boxley*	
	Garcia going blind. Should try to call Mrs...	Writing
11.30–	Barrymore sick and breaking down. He'll	
12.00	play it if we have to change the script and (8)	acting
	put the hero in an iron lung	
	Find out about occulist	
12.00–	*Tough Conference inc. Jackie on the roof.*	
12.30	*Takes the gloom out of a picture and gives it*	
	style. The scram business. No Trace of girl An	Planning
	agent	
12.30–		(9)
1.00		
1.00–1.30	COMMISSARY—Hunch about Garcia (10)	Policy
1.30–2.00		
2.00–2.30	Musa Dagh—Consul	Policy
	Details about women	
2.30–3.00		
3.00–3.30	RUSHES (11)	Cutting
3.30–4.00		

	Finds out it's Smith	
4.00–4.30	Process Stuff on Stage ???	Acting
4.30–5.00	Happy Ending with Brady	Policy
	The Occulist calls	
5.00–5.30	The Marquands	Writing
	The Phone Call	
5.30–6.00	Avoiding someone	
	Leading actresses for Long Beach	Extra
6.00–6.30	Problem of Russia. Symbolic. Fatigue	Writing
6.30–7.30	More rushes. Well earned rest. Dubbing room	Cutting
7.30–7.45	*Pedro Garcia*	Personal
7.45–8.30	Dinner	
9.00–00	Starts Out missing Dubbing	

The twelve-page holograph draft (A) introduces Prince Agge [3] to whom Stahr explains that a problem has arisen because a husband-and-wife writing team, the Marquands, have discovered that other writers are also working on their script. During this conversation with Agge Stahr makes the statement, " 'I'm the unity.' " In the ribbon (C) and carbon (B) copies Fitzgerald cancelled the meeting between Stahr and Agge, replacing it with the beginning of the conference between Stahr and the English writer Boxley.

A key event in episode 7 is the announcement that the cameraman Pedro Garcia (Pete Zavras) has attempted suicide. The notes indicate that he was to play an important role at the end of the novel by warning Stahr of Brady's plots. On page 3 of the revised typescript and carbon copy for episode 7 Miss Doolan's report on Garcia is lined out: " 'Yes, Mr. Stahr. I called about Pedro Garcia—he tried to kill himself in front of Warner Brothers last week. Mr. Brown says he's going blind . . . I've got Joe Wyman—about the trousers.' " Fitzgerald noted in the margin, "Dots don't properly separate ideas." But in episode 9 Stahr refers to Garcia's "eye-trouble," although no source is provided for the information. Since it is unlikely that Fitzgerald intended to omit this information, a possible explanation is that he crossed out Miss Doolan's speech in order to revise it but neglected to do so.

Episode 8

A   Manuscript & Revised Typescript. 1–5, 4, 5–13. "Episode 9"
B   Revised Carbon Copy. 1–9. "Episode 9 [8"
C   Revised Typescript. 1–9 "Episode 9 [8." *Latest Typescript.*

Outline

8. First Conference

Episode 8 (originally marked episode 9) consists of 3 segments: a holograph draft with 3 revised typescript inserts (A), and the revised ribbon (C) and carbon (B) copies. The typed inserts in the holograph indicate that it conflates at least two layers of writing, as Fitzgerald inserted material from rejected episode 9. Episode 8 describes Stahr's meetings with Boxley and the impotent actor— separated by the comic interlude of gagman Mike Van Dyke demonstrating a slapstick movie routine for Boxley. The episode ends with the opening of Stahr's script conference with White, Broaca, Rienmund, and Rose Meloney.

Beginning with the ribbon copy for episode 8 the symbol *re* (possibly *rl*) appears on the top page of the typescript of several episodes. The meaning of this symbol is not certain, but Frances Kroll Ring, Fitzgerald's secretary, thinks it stood for "rewrite." If so, then it is certain that Fitzgerald regarded the latest typescripts as work that was still developing.

Rejected Episode 9

A   Manuscript. 1–7. "Episode 9"
B   Revised Carbon Copy. 1–4. "Episode 9"
C   Typescript. 1–4. "Episode 9"

Rejected episode 9—which corresponds to outline episode 8— survives in holograph, typescript, and incompletely revised carbon copy. In rejected episode 9 Stahr takes Mike Van Dyke and Prince Agge to a script conference with producer Lee Spurgeon and a husband-and-wife writing team, the Marquands. Fitzgerald's original plan was to have Agge spend the whole day with Stahr and observe all of his meetings, thereby enabling Cecelia to cite Agge as the source for her account of Stahr's working day.

After cancelling this episode, Fitzgerald added to episode 8 the scene of Van Dyke demonstrating a slapstick routine for Boxley. In episode 10 there is a deleted comment (probably deleted by Edmund Wilson) that Popolous' speech reminds Agge of Van Dyke's double talk. As was noted in a cancelled part of episode 7, the Marquands are upset because other writers are working on their assignment. Stahr bluffs them by telling them he has assigned them to another script, to which they respond by asking to be kept on the original movie. Stahr leaves Van Dyke in the script conference to insult Spurgeon as a way to placate the Marquands. At the head of the carbon copy Fitzgerald noted: "OUT Double talk doesn't jell. Whole thing confused. Name Lee Spurgeon." This rejected episode shows Stahr as a manipulator, rather than displaying his ability to work with writers.

[Segment C]

900 words

EPISODE 9

In front of the door of the bungalow doing nothing stood a dark saucer-eyed man.

"Hello, Monroe."

"Hello, Mike," said Monroe. He introduced him to the visitor, "Prince Agge, this is Mr. Van Dyke. You've laughed at his stuff many times. He's the best gag-man in pictures."

"In the world," said the saucer-eyed man gravely, "—the funniest man in the world. How are you, Prince?"

"Mike, I can use you," said Stahr, "I've got a rebellion on in Lee Spurgeon's office and I want to keep the lid on for a day. Just gang up with me for a few minutes."

He went ahead frowning a little and during the short walk the

Prince found himself engaged in conversation with Mike Van Dyke. He answered politely without quite getting the jist of the words. Something about the commissary where Mr. Van Dyke thought he had seen the prince trying to order what sounded like twisted fish and a cat's handlebar, though the Prince was certain he misunderstood.

He tried to explain that he had not been to the commissary but by this time they were so far into the subject that he thought it quickest to admit that he had and merely parry Mr. Van Dyke's mistaken statements of what he had done there. Mr. Van Dyke was not so much insistent as convinced and he seemed to talk very fast.

They were inside and the Prince was introduced to Mr. Spurgeon and to Mr. and Mrs. Marquand but he was now so involved in the conversation with Mr. Van Dyke that he heard himself stammering I'm glad to meet me because he was explaining to Van Dyke that he had *not* seen Technigarbo in Grettacolor. Again he had misunderstood. Was his name Albert Edward Butch Arthur Agge David, Prince of Denmark. That's my cousin, he almost said, his head reeling.

Stahr's voice, clear and reassuring, brought him back to reality.

"That's enough, Mike. That was 'double-talk,' he explained to Prince Agge. It's considered funny here in the lower brackets. Do it slow, Mike."

Mike demonstrated politely.

"In an income at the gate this morning—" He pointed at Stahr, "—did he?"

Baffled the Dane bit again.

"What? Did he what?" Then he smiled, "I see. It is like your Gertrude Stein."

Mike Van Dyke subsided. Prince Agge looked at the three inhabitants of the room, all sulky with what was on their minds. The little eager man and his squat wife were obviously wanting to speak up but harrassed by the presence of strangers. Spurgeon, a blonde German Jew who stood behind his desk laughing obediently for Stahr, spoke up.

"Monroe, we have several things—"

"So have I," interrupted Stahr, suddenly serious. His tone was that of a popular young headmaster, pleasant, firm, intent. The Dane saw that it evoked a complementary mood in the listeners.

"I've read the work you sent over and I think Mr. and Mrs. Marquand are going to be very valuable to us. In fact I'm taking them away from you, Lee."

He had them—all three of them. His words brought their tensity down to a plane of quiet.

"I'm sorry because I liked the scenes—especially the ones on the bus from 6 to 13A." He turned courteously to the woman as if he had read her handwriting through the typescript. "It was fresh and new."

"It was my husband's scene," said Mrs. Marquand quickly.

"It was a fine scene." He looked at Lee Spurgeon, "Keep it just as it is. I need the Marquands on another story—something we don't have to get on the screen so quick."

A short silence.

"But we like the story—" began Marquand, "It's only that—"

"I must go," said Stahr. His eye flickered surreptitiously at Van Dyke. "Come and see me tomorrow at noon."

Mike Van Dyke stepped into the breech, addressing the two hesitant Marquands.

"Does Lee ever go 'Bang!—Bang!—Bang!?'" he inquired maliciously, striking his palm with his clenched fist. "You know: 'And then the girl burns up bang! and then the man breaks out bang! and then the sky falls bang! And then we get Bang! Bang! Bang! If he hasn't sold you that he hasn't given you the old fashioned seed-corn prester m'chester."

He had some grudge against Spurgeon and he was taking full advantage of an opportunity. Stahr had turned away, cocking back a watchful eye.

"He has a beginning too—watch for it. Once when he was a kid he looked through a fence and saw a rich girl with big dogs jumping around her. If you ever want to sell him something have a big dog in it. Have it jump on a girl."

Stahr and the Prince were out now but as the door closed they heard the jester continuing inside, intoxicated with his ecstatic moment of power.

"Or else have a rich girl go into a stable and slap a horse on the rump—"

Out in the timid California noon Stahr stuck his hands deep in his pocket and frowned.

"Those Marquands are good people—I can't let them go."

"You're putting them to another picture."

"No—tomorrow they'll ask to stay on this."

"Even with other people writing it too."

Stahr nodded.

"It'll be all right. It's only that Spurgeon handles writers badly. He doesn't know which ones need a firm hand and which ones don't. People like the Marquands would pack up and get out tomorrow. Spurgeon doesn't know what pride is—there's not much of it around here."

But looking at Stahr Prince Agge was not at all sure this was true.

Episode 9

A   Manuscript & Revised Typescript. 1–19 "Episode 10 [9"
B   Revised Carbon Copy. 1–11 "Episode 9"
C   Revised Typescript. 1–11 "Episode 9" *Latest Typescript*

Outline

9.   Second conference and afterwards.

Episode 9 (originally marked episode 10) survives in three drafts: a holograph draft with one page of revised typescript (A), and the revised ribbon (C) and carbon (B) copies. This episode, which replaces rejected episode 9, presents a much more impressive view of Stahr in a script conference with Broaca, Rienmund, White, and Rose Meloney. The description of Rose Meloney at the end of episode 8 is repeated in episode 9; it was deleted in the second appearance, probably by Wilson. (See Sheilah Graham's 11 January 1941 letter to Maxwell Perkins in Chapter 6 below.) Here Stahr functions brilliantly, explaining to the group how to rewrite their script. The conference is followed by a conversation between Stahr and his secretary, Miss Doolan, about tracing the girls in the flood and about Pedro Garcia's suicide attempt. The ribbon typescript has the note "[   ] re but transfer last page to end of Episode 7"—indicating that Stahr's conversation with Miss Doolan about the girl wearing the silver belt was to follow his first attempt to trace the women. The episode was to end with the words, "The conference was over."

Wilson interpolated into the end of episode 9 a brief scene salvaged from rejected episode 10 in which Agge is with Stahr when a misconnected call from Marcus comes through to Stahr. (This scene appears on pp. 43–44 of the first edition of *The Last Tycoon*.) There is no compelling reason for inserting this material in episode 9, apart from showing the impression Stahr makes on the Danish Prince—who has not appeared in the novel at this point (Agge had been introduced in rejected episode 9). It is possible that Fitzgerald intended to use misconnected phone calls as a symbolic device—see the call between Brady and the New York office that Stahr hears in the cancelled portion of Chapter II. The idea was apparently dropped—or at least refined. There is a good deal of telephoning in the novel, but that is natural for Stahr.

REJECTED EPISODE 10

A   Manuscript. 8–18, insert 18 1–3, 19. "Episode 10"
B   Carbon Copy. 1–11. "Episode 10."
C   Carbon Copy. 1–11. "Episode 10"

A rejected first draft of episode 10—which corresponds to outline episode 9—survives in holograph (A) and two carbons (B & C). It covers Miss Doolan's reports on the girl's name and Garcia's eyesight, Stahr's script conference with Broaca and White, the misconnected call from Marcus, Miss Doolan's second reports on the girl and Garcia, and Pops Carlson's slapstick routine. Fitzgerald stripped one of the carbons of the slapstick material which he then incorporated in episode 9—renaming Carlson Mike Van Dyke. There is an important difference between this rejected version of the script conference and the revised version: in the rejected version Stahr is shown blundering:

[Segment C]

"And that's no good about the child playing with the loaded revolver. It's lousy."

The Dane saw White and Broaca exchange a glance. Stahr saw it too.

"Well, it is," he said, "I'm not going to waste a good morning saying why. Get something else there—I had a—"

Wylie laughed suddenly. Politely and maliciously he took a sheet from his folio and gave it to Stahr.

"Orders of the old master," he said, "You went for it. Here's the note."

Stahr looked at the paper angrily.

"I had a lapse," he said. "It's an uncomfortable scene. What I was thinking—"

There is no comparable material in any of the latest typescripts, for Stahr is always right and has no memory lapses or errors in judgment.

,

Episode 10

A   Manuscript. 1–11. "Episode 11"
B   Carbon Copy. 1–7. "Episode 11 [10"
C   Revised Typescript. 1–7. "Episode 11 [10." *Latest Typescript*

Outline

10. Commissary and Idealism about non-profit pictures. Rushes. Phone call, etc.

Episode 10 (originally marked episode 11) exists in three layers: holograph (A), and revised ribbon (C) and unrevised carbon (B) copies. The first page of the ribbon copy has this note: "re except for last page; transfer?" And at the head of the carbon copy Fitzgerald wrote, "Dramatize and make clear." This episode describes the lunch that Stahr and Agge attended with the studio executives. The holograph breaks off with the group's reaction to Stahr's announcement that he intends to make an unprofitable movie; it is augmented in the typescript by Agge's reaction to the actor made up as Lincoln and Miss Doolan's report on the search for the girl in the flood. Agge's Lincoln epiphany was salvaged from a rejected version of episode 12 (See Episode 10 Continuation), and provides one of the elements in the presidential theme that Fitzgerald appears to have been developing. The last page of episode 10 that Fitzgerald considered transferring covers Stahr's return to his office after lunch and Miss Doolan's report that Robinson remembers one of the women in the flood was named Smith.

EPISODE 10 CONTINUATION

A   Manuscript. 1, 1a, 1b, 1c, 2–5. "Episode 12 (1st part)"
B   Carbon Copy. 1–5. "Episode 12 (1st part)"
C   Revised Typescript & Manuscript. 7–10. "Episode 10 Continuation"

Rejected episode 10 (originally marked episode 12) survives in three layers—a holograph (A), a carbon copy (B), and the heavily revised typescript (C) that Fitzgerald headed "Episode 10 Continuation" and had retyped. The existence of rejected or dismantled episodes indicates that Fitzgerald tried to solve structural problems by shifting scenes.

Segments (A) and (B) describe Agge's reaction to the Lincoln actor at the conclusion of the executives' lunch, which is followed by Stahr's phone call setting up the meeting with the wrong girl. In (C) the Lincoln material is followed by Miss Doolan's report that one of the girls at the flood was named Smith. Segment (C) was incorporated in episode 10.

Episodes 10 and 11 depart from Fitzgerald's outline. The phone call to the wrong girl planned for episode 10 was moved to episode 11. The outline calls for two scenes showing Stahr viewing the rushes—in episodes 10 and 11—but there is only the one such scene, in episode 11.

Insert for Episode 10

A   Manuscript. [1] 2–6. "Episode 10 [For Episode 10"
B   Carbon Copy. 1, 1–4. "For Episode 10 [11"
C   Revised Typescript. 1, 1–4. "For Episode 10." *Latest Typescript*

The scene in which Stahr replaces director Red Ridingwood—not noted in Fitzgerald's outline—consists of the holograph (A) and the revised carbon (B) and ribbon copies (C)—with two versions of the paragraph describing Stahr's arrival on the set. Fitzgerald was dissatisfied with this insert material, noting at the head of the ribbon copy: "No good—I think OUT." Another memo shows what bothered him: "What is missing in the Ridingwood scene is passion and imagination, etc. What an extraordinary thing that it should all have been there for Ridingwood and not there." The Ridingwood insert opens with Stahr arriving on Ridingwood's set and ends with their departure; but it is not linked up with the rest of the episode. Wilson incorporated the Ridingwood scene in episode 11 as the opening of Chapter 4, but it is by no means clear that it is properly positioned—or that it really should be retained in the novel.

Episode 11

A   Manuscript & Revised Typescript. [1]–21. "Episode 11"
B   Revised Carbon Copy. 1–13. "Episode 11"
C   Revised Typescript. 1–13. "Episode 11." *Latest Typescript*

Outline

D.   11 Visit to rushes

Episode 11 exists in 3 forms: the holograph with interpolated typescript (A), and the revised ribbon (C) and revised carbon (B) copies. The episode was written in two parts. Holograph pages 1–11 cover Stahr's work in the projection room viewing rushes and screentests. The second part (pages 12–21), summarizes Stahr's work from 6 P.M. to dinner, including Pedro Garcia's (Zavras) visit to thank him for stopping the rumor about the cameraman's failing sight and ending with Stahr blacking out from fatigue. It includes five pages of interpolated typescript for the discussion between Stahr and Agge about writers (page 12) and Stahr's phone conversation with the wrong girl from Episode 10 Continuation (pages 14–17). Page 12 has Stahr's statement, "I'm the unity"—moved from episode 7. Coming here after the reader has seen him at work, Stahr's claim seems justified.

Fitzgerald was not satisfied with this episode; and the revised ribbon copy has his note: "Cut first 8 pages—then continue cut from foot of 11 to end." If these cuts were made, only the phone conversation with the girl would be left from episode 11; but it seems highly unlikely that Fitzgerald did not plan to replace this important material with another report of Stahr's afternoon and evening, for the novel requires a full account of Stahr's long working day. Perhaps the new material would have included the Ridingwood scene.

EPISODE 12

A   Manuscript. 1–10, 10½, 11. "Episode 13"
B   Carbon Copy. 1–5. "Episode 13"
C   Revised Typescript. 1–5. "Episode 13"

D   Carbon Copy. 1–5. "Episode 13"
E   Revised Typescript & Manuscript. 1–11. "Episode 13"

F   Carbon Copy. 1–8. "Episode 13 [12"
G   Revised Typescript. 1–8. "Episode 13 [12" *Latest Typescript*

Outline

12. Second Meeting that night.
     Wrong girl—glimpse

Since episode 12 was originally episode 13, it is barely possible that a discarded episode 12 preceded it—See Episode 10 Continuation. Some support for this guess is provided by the one-page "End of 12" discussed below, which does not really fit the end of this episode 12 and may have been the conclusion for another episode. Episode 12 as it exists here does conform to Fitzgerald's outline; however, the last outline was probably drawn up *after* Fitzgerald had made substantial progress on the novel and incorporates some structural decisions that had already been written into the novel.

Episode 12 survives in three separate levels of writing: the holograph first draft (A) with its typescripts (B & C), the second typescript (D & E), and the third typescript (F & G). The second ribbon copy (E) was extended by eight pages of holograph which report Stahr's second meeting with Kathleen (who is here named Nora) after his date with the wrong girl; this draft was then retyped and revised into the latest typescript (G). Episode 12 required special attention and extra work because Fitzgerald had to establish the attraction that Stahr and Kathleen have for each other at their first real meeting. That Fitzgerald was concerned about making Kathleen's effect on Stahr convincing is shown by the note already referred to: "Where will the warmth come from in this. Why does he think she's warm. Warmer than the voice in Farewell. My girls were all so warm and full of promise. The sea at night. What can I do to make it honest and different?"

The episode closes with Stahr's return to his lonely home and his longing for his dead Minna (a name that echoes *Norma* and *Zelda)*: "When he took up the first of two scripts that were his evening stint, that presently he would visualize line by line on the screen, he waited a moment, thinking of Minna. He explained to her that it was really nothing, that no one could ever be like she was, that he was sorry."

END OF EPISODE 12

A Manuscript. [1] "End of 12"
B Carbon Copy. [1]
C Typescript. [1]

[Segment C]

That was substantially a day of Stahr's. I don't know about the illness when it started, etc., because he was secretive but I know he fainted a couple of times that month because Father told me. Prince Agge is my authority for the luncheon in the commissary where he told them he was going to make a picture that would lose money— which was something considering the men he had to deal with and that he held a big block of stock and had a profit sharing contract.

And Wylie White told me a lot which I believed because he felt Stahr intensely with a mixture of jealousy and admiration. As for me I was head over heels in love with him then and you can take what I say for what it's worth.

Wilson placed this page at the end of episode 12—after Stahr's thoughts about his dead wife, but it blunts the moving conclusion of the episode. Cecelia cites Agge and White as the sources for her account of Stahr's day; but neither of them could have told her about Stahr's meeting with Kathleen, which strongly suggests that this "End of 12" page belongs with the account of Stahr's working day. The attempt in this passage to remind the reader that the story is being told from Cecelia's point of view, with help from other sources, calls attention to the narrative problem in the novel: Cecelia was proving to be too limited as a narrator. In his prospectus for Littauer Fitzgerald had explained: "That is to say by making Cecelia, at the moment of her telling the story, an intelligent and observant woman, I shall grant myself the privilege, as Conrad did, of letting her imagine the actions of the characters. Thus, I hope to get the verisimilitude of a first person narrative, combined with a Godlike knowledge of all events that happen to my characters." After episode 12 Fitzgerald tells more and more of the story himself, omitting Cecelia's attempts to document the scenes she does not witness. Fitzgerald planned *The Last Tycoon* on the model of *The Great Gatsby*, with Cecelia having more narrative freedom than Nick Carraway. The plan did not work because *The Last Tycoon* involves so much action that Cecelia cannot witness or even document. In *Gatsby*, for example, Fitzgerald provided no account of what transpired between Daisy and Gatsby in the meetings after their reunion. But in *The Last Tycoon* the reader is given intimate reports of meetings between Stahr and Kathleen at which no one else is present.

EPISODE 13

A Manuscript. 1–11. "13 (1st part)"
B Carbon Copy. 1–6. "Episode 13"
C Revised Typescript. 1–6. "Episode 13." *Latest Typescript*

D Manuscript. 1–5, 5½, 6–16. "13 (continued)"
E Carbon Copy. 1–9. "13 (continued)"
F Revised Typescript. 1–9. "13 (continued)." *Latest Typescript*

Outline

E 13. Cecelia and Stahr and Ball—Aug. 6th Football game. Cecelia and Wylie and Maude.

Episode 13 (the opening of Wilson's Chapter 5) was written in two parts: 1) "13 (1st part)"—Cecelia's conversation with Wylie on her way to see Stahr, and her brief meeting with Stahr in which she offers him her love (A–C); 2) "13 (continued)"— the screenwriters' ball at which Stahr encounters Kathleen (D–F) again. The two parts are not linked. That Fitzgerald was not satisfied with the first part is indicated by his note at the head of the revised typescript: "Not too hot," with the "re" symbol crossed out.

At one point Fitzgerald planned to continue episode 13 with a football game scene, as confirmed by one of his notes: "A football game on a blazing hot July day. Two hot teams messing around at $500 a day. Actors, extras and a camera crew. High in the empty stadium, Stahr and his girl."

According to Fitzgerald's notes, the character Maude was a Bennington friend of Cecelia's: "Cecelia has Maude with her who is to present her Philly. Has the girl coming for the summer."

Fitzgerald dropped this character—probably because he felt that the novel was overpopulated—and nothing survives about Maude.

SECTION 14

A Manuscript. 1–6, insert 6, 7–13, 13½. "Section 14"
B Manuscript. 8–11. "(Attach to Section 14, Part I)"
C Carbon Copy. 1–10. "Section 14"
D Revised Typescript. 1–10. "Section 14" *Latest Typescript*

E Manuscript. 1–9. "Section 14 (2nd part)"
F Carbon Copy. 1–4. "Section 14 (2nd part)"
G Revised Typescript. "Section 14 (2nd part)" *Latest Typescript*

H Manuscript [1] 2–15 [16–25], 12–18, 18½, 19, 20, 20½, 21–23. "Section 14 (Part III)"
K Carbon Copy. 1–17. "Section 14 (Part III)"
I Revised Typescript. 11
J Carbon Copy. 11–13
L Revised Typescript. 1–17 "Section 14 (Part III)" *Latest Typescript*

Outline

14. Malibu seduction. Try to get on lot.
    DEAD MIDDLE.

It does not seem meaningful that for sections 14 and 15 Fitzgerald changed from the designation *episode* to *section*—that is, there is no indication that he differentiated between the terms. Section 14 is unusually long, but section 15 is of normal episode length.

Section 14 was written in 3 parts: 1) Stahr's date with Kathleen up to the orang-outang phone call (A–D); 2) "Section 14 (2nd part)"—the drive from Malibu to Kathleen's house (E–G); 3) "Section 14 (Part 3)—the return to Malibu through the love-making and Stahr's arrival home (H–L).

Fitzgerald was dissatisfied with the pacing of the first part of section 14, as indicated by his note on the typescript: "Criticism—time lapse not good. No drawing together." The holograph shows that Fitzgerald wrote the opening up to the orang-outang call and turned it over to his secretary while he worked on the call: "(Phone scene to be invented. Much slower—the hunt ect + more significant." The account of this call was written as a four-page sequence (B) and added to the first part. The orang-outang material does not really succeed. Stahr becomes humanized for Kathleen when she sees him in a ridiculous circumstance; nonetheless, the scene is neither convincing nor necessary. In the holograph (A) Stahr's unfinished beach house is first described as a "skeleton," which is changed to "fusilage." With this small revision Fitzgerald reinforced the idea of elevation associated with Stahr: even his home is like something designed for flight.

The four-page second part (E) presented no difficulties; but the long love sequence that completes section 14 required three holograph installments (H). The first installment is fifteen pages describing the love-making up to Stahr's announcement that it is the night of the grunion. Fitzgerald was obviously making symbolic use of the grunion. That the fish die in order to spawn is a reminder that Stahr, who has just made love to Kathleen, is dying. The second installment of ten unnumbered holograph pages ([16–25]) describes the meeting with the Negro who doesn't approve of movies and the drive back through Stahr's reading of Kathleen's letter. An important difference in the treatment of the letter is that in the holograph (H) Kathleen puts it behind the seat of the car and tells Stahr where to find it, but in the typescript (L) she accidentally drops the letter in the car where it is found by Stahr's butler. This difference indicates that Fitzgerald altered his conception of Kathleen's attitude toward Stahr. In the holograph she still intends to break off with Stahr— even after making love with him—for she tells him where to find the letter terminating their relationship. But in the typescript Kathleen thinks she has lost the letter, which she says "doesn't matter." She is uncertain now about her plans and accepts the accident of the lost letter as an excuse to delay breaking off with Stahr. The change is very important, for it converts the impression of section 14 from one of futility to possibility. After the third installment was typed, Fitzgerald wrote a longer conclusion in holograph, pages 12–23 (H), keyed to carbon pages 12–13 (J) that were being replaced. In the process of expanding the conclusion of section 14 Fitzgerald rewrote Kathleen's letter, which he noted in the first typescript "lacks style." The original letter is wordy; it says more than is necessary in discussing her future husband and in asking Stahr to pretend not to know her should they meet.

[Segment J]

He got into bed picked up the top script from the pile on his night table and looked at the title. Then he put it down and opened the letter. (This letter wrong)

Dear Mr. Stahr:

I am going to give you this letter when we say goodbye tonight. I am going to give it to you because I have found you are hard to say goodbye to—so I will pretend we are going to meet again and give you this letter.

Naturally I am impressed by your liking me. As I write my hostess of last night has just left, after telling me for an hour what a great man you are. (I think I am supposed to tell you she thinks so. So give her a job if you can.) I am impressed no end.

And now I'll tell you why I can't meet you again. I didn't come to California for nothing—I came to meet the man whom I am going to marry. He is just a plain citizen who is not going to be an important man like you but his work is here and we are going to live here and naturally it would not please him to know I had already met such a "big shot," visited Mr. Stahr's studio etc., before he arrived. He would be (a) possibly suspicious and (b) his pride would be hurt.

So there we are. I can't see you any more. I am not free—I am extremely and definitely and finally committed to devote myself to another man. If you are still fascinated please recover—if not then so much the better. When I say I'm sorry it has to be this way it is not to lead you on but to acknowledge frankly that I find you attractive. But that is emphatically all. I have had five tumultous years that were about one fifth ecstacy to four fifths misery and I want to settle down as a good wife and a real person.

You don't fit in the picture—we will move in different spheres and I would a little rather that if we should meet we pretend not to recognize each other. That is the understanding with myself upon which I am going out with you this afternoon. It is difficult to ask you to forget now that we ever met.

In All Friendliness
KATHLEEN MOORE

(letter lacks style)

This is the rewritten letter.

Dear Mr. Stahr.

In half an hour I will be keeping my date with you. When we say goodbye I will hand you this letter. It is to tell you that I am to be married soon and that I won't be able to see you after today.

I should have told you last night but it didn't seem to concern you. And it would seem silly to spend this beautiful afternoon telling you about it and watching your interest fade. Let it fade all at once—now. I will have told you enough to convince you that I am Nobody's Prize Potato. (I have just learned that expression—from my hostess of last night who called and stayed an hour. She seems to believe that everyone is Nobody's Prize Potato—except you. I think I am supposed to tell you she thinks this, so give her a job if you can.)

I am very flattered that anyone who sees so many lovely women I can't finish this sentence but you know what I mean. And I will be late if I don't go to meet you right now.

With All Good Wishes
Kathleen Moore.

The expansion of the conclusion for section 14 was partly prompted by criticisms Fitzgerald received from Sheilah Graham and Frances Kroll, as recorded in this memo: "Sheilah and Frances hate the letter and both miss more emotion or something after seduction. The talk about Edna seems cold. They would like to develop negro and Stahr's reaction. They do not understand that the girl is not in the market—suspect her of leading him on. But he must not know the truth so perhaps the reader should."

The expanded conclusion of section 14 postpones Stahr's reading of Kathleen's letter by some three hours as Fitzgerald analyzes Stahr's reactions to his day with Kathleen. Perhaps prompted by the criticisms of Miss Graham and Miss Kroll, Fitzgerald has Stahr change the studio's production schedule in response to his conversation with the Negro on the beach. Stahr deliberately delays reading Kathleen's letter to show himself that he is still in control of the situation; and Fitzgerald notes that sexual passion has had no place in Stahr's life—explaining that although he grew up "cold," he "had learned tolerance, kindness, forebearance, and even affection like lessons." Fitzgerald was unable to complete his analysis, leaving a note in the latest typescript: "(Now the idea about young and generous)."

After rewriting the conclusion to section 14, Fitzgerald remained uncertain about it, for he wrote at the end of the holograph: "Comment: This may not be terse and clear enough here. Or perhaps I mean strong enough. It may be the place for the doctor's verdict. I would like to leave him on a stronger note." The doctor's examination comes in episode 16, where Dr. Baer recognizes that Stahr "was due to die very soon now." Fitzgerald's reason for considering moving the doctor scene to the end of section 14 was to emphasize the sense of love and death surrounding Stahr and Kathleen. Without Kathleen to make him ease up, Stahr will die in a matter of months.

The outline shows that at one point Fitzgerald planned to follow the Malibu seduction with a scene in which Stahr tries to take Kathleen into the studio, and the notes indicate that they were to be turned away by a studio guard who does not recognize Stahr. The scene does not survive in any form and was probably never drafted. "DEAD MIDDLE" means that episode was the emotional center of the novel, the still point before the plot complications develop.

SECTION 15

A   Manuscript. 1–2, 2½, 3–7. "Section 15 (first part)"
B   Carbon Copy. 1–4. "Section 15 (first part)"
C   Revised Typescript. 1–4. "Section 15 (first part)" *Latest Typescript*

D   Manuscript. 1–8. "15. (Second part)"
E   Carbon Copy. 1–5. "15 (second part)"
F   Revised Typescript. 1–5. "15 (second part)" *Latest Typescript*

Outline

15. Cecelia and father

Fitzgerald wrote section 15 in two parts: Cecelia's visit with Rose Meloney to ask her to arrange a meeting with Martha Dodd at which Cecelia will try to find out about Kathleen (A–C); and the lunch with Martha, followed by Cecelia's discovery of the naked secretary in her father's office (D–F). Section 15 opens with the sentence, "This is Cecelia taking up the story," which some critics have cited as clumsy (as is said about "To resume Rosemary's point of view" in *Tender Is the Night*). This instruction to the reader comes after a long section which Cecelia does not narrate. Although the question of what Fitzgerald would have done about the narrator in subsequent revisions must remain moot, it is clear he had discovered that Cecelia's narration did not permit sufficient scope for the action of the novel.

Fitzgerald was not satisfied with section 15. At the head of the typescript for the first part he made this cryptic note: "re except if continues C's role in story"; and at the head of the second part he wrote "Not very good."

In assembling the material for this edition of *The Last Tycoon*, Edmund Wilson numbered the pages of Fitzgerald's latest typescripts 1–182. The last page of section 14 is page 140; but Wilson then continued with the start of episode 16 as page 141—with section 15 moved to a position after episode 17 as pages 174–182. This transportation of episodes was corrected in the setting copy. Wilson's original ordering is baffling, since the content of section 15 clearly places it between section 14 and episode 16. Wilson's problem in positioning section 15 appears to be related to his incertainty about handling episode 16. He first designated episode 16 as the opening of Chapter 6 but then made episode 17 the chapter opening.

EPISODE 16

A   Manuscript. [1] 2–5. "Episode 16, 1st Part"
B   Carbon Copy. 1–4. "Episode 16, First Part"
C   Revised Typescript. 1–4. "Episode 16, First Part" *Latest Typescript*

D   Manuscript. [1] 2–5, 5½, 6–15, 15½, 16–21. "Episode 16 (Part 2)"
E   Carbon Copy. 1–12. "Episode 16 (Part 2)"
F   Revised Typescript. 1–12. "Episode 16 (Part 2)" *Latest Typescript*

Outline

16.   Phone call & Wedding.

Episode 16 was also written in two parts: 1) the scene in which Boxley begins to function as a screenwriter, with Stahr's invention of the coin-tossing game at the deadlocked script conference (A–C); 2) and the electrocardiograph examination of Stahr at which Dr. Baer privately predicts Stahr's imminent death, followed by Stahr's phone call from Kathleen and their date during which she tells him about her past as a mistress of a deposed king (D–F). Fitzgerald noted at the head of the episode: "re except for the picture of Stahr at work."

Kathleen's comparison of her king with Stahr here is noteworthy: "But he wasn't much like a king. Not nearly as much as you." Stahr's regality has been previously indicated in the novel, notably at the end of Chapter 1 when he is described as Napoleonic and is called "the last of the princes." On first consideration these references seem to clash with the theme of Stahr's American-ness— Stahr as the self-made man whose career fulfills the promises of American life. But Fitzgerald is indicating that the great Americans constitute an aristocracy of aspiration and achievement. He was intensely patriotic, and was moved by America's history. Among the notes for the novel is this pondering: "I look out at it—and I think it is the most beautiful history in the world. It is the history of me and of my people. And if I came here yesterday like Sheilah I should still think so. It is the history of all aspiration—not just the American dream but the human dream and if I came at the end of it that too is a place in the line of the pioneers."

At the end of the second part Stahr makes his terrible mistake in deciding to wait until the next day before going away with Kathleen. Here Fitzgerald takes a great risk by revealing his climax in advance with a chorus-like exhortation:

[Segment F]

. . . It is your chance, Stahr. Better take it now. This is your girl. She can save you, she can worry you back to life. She will take looking after and you will grow strong to do it. But take her now—tell her and take her away. Neither of you know it but far away over the night The American has changed his plans. At this moment his train is speeding through Albuquerque; the schedule is accurate. The engineer is on time. In the morning he will be here.

Fitzgerald's gamble succeeds brilliantly; the warning gives the reader a sense of foreknowledge, thereby making Stahr's hesitation all the more terrible and tragic. The episode ends with Kathleen's telegram informing Stahr that she has just been married.

EPISODE 17

A   Manuscript. 1–4, 4½, 5–6, 6½, 7–8, 8½, 9¿ 9½, 10–15, 15½, 16, 17, (insert), 17½, 18–26. "Episode 17"

B   Carbon Copy. 1–17. "Episode 17"
C   Revised Typescript. 1–17. "Episode 17." *Latest Typescript*

Outline

F   17. The Damn breaks with Brimmer

The last work Fitzgerald did on the novel in December 1940 was episode 17 (the opening of Wilson's Chapter 6), which survives in holograph and typescript. But there was a lost revision between the manuscript and the typescript. The head of the typescript has the "re" or "rl" symbol. This episode covering Stahr's meeting with the communist organizer has two functions: to develop Stahr's ideas about the Screenwriters' Guild and to show the effect Kathleen's marriage has had on Stahr. Budd Schulberg recalls "the Brimmer character is based on an actual communist organizer that Maurice Rapf and I knew in Hollywood. I was discussing this with Maurice recently and he remembers telling Scott about the ping-pong scene involving his father Harry Rapf, one of the established producers at MGM in the Thalberg era." [4]

Speaking through Cecelia, Fitzgerald analyzes Stahr's political conservatism before his meeting with Brimmer. The original holograph version is:

[Segment A]

If Stahr had been a religious man these attractions might [   ] have cut deep into him but he was a rationalist who did his own reasoning without benefit of books—and he had just managed to climb out of a thousand years of Jewry into the late the eighteenth century. He did not want to throw it away. He had a dramatists respect for structure too, and none of this was included in the fantasy of his life. He cherished a parvenu's passionate loyalty to an imaginary past.

This analysis was tightened in the missing revision that preceded the typescript.

Although Fitzgerald partly attributes Stahr's politics—or lack of them—to his "climb out of a thousand years of Jewry," his Jewishness is not emphasized. In his 1939 plan for Kenneth Littauer,

Fitzgerald noted, "The racial angle shall scarcely be touched on at all." It is simply an obvious fact that Stahr is a Jew. The first clear reference to Stahr's Jewish background does not come until the Malibu scene of section 14, when his distress at Kathleen's wasted education is explained in terms of "a racial memory of the old schules."

Stahr has no stereotypical Jewish characteristics; and Fitzgerald's notes show that he omitted material based on Stahr's Jewishness—for example, a projected scene in which Stahr would tell a movie plot in Yiddish. In the novel Stahr's speech is free from Yiddishisms. Indeed, he may be too goyish.

Fitzgerald does not ignore or conceal the Jewish aspects of Hollywood in the thirties. In the commissary scene he notes that most of the men at table are Jews, but makes a point of refuting the assumption that all Jews are financial wizards. Fitzgerald, however, did believe that Jews are emotionally more intense than Gentiles, and that the Jews determined Hollywood's mood. As he noted: "Cling to reality, for any departure from a high pitch of reality at which the Jews live leads to a farce in which the Christians live. Hollywood is a Jewish holiday, a gentiles tragedy."

A boss who believes in total responsibility, Stahr opposes the Guild because he sees it as a violation of subordination, a dilution of the unity he had achieved—and because he does not think that writers are equipped for authority. Fitzgerald is not satirizing Stahr in giving him a statement like this: "Writers are children—even in normal times they can't keep their minds on their work." Although Fitzgerald did not share Stahr's views of writers, he understood why Stahr held them. If Stahr is an anchronism, he is a magnificent anachronism.

The effect on Stahr of the loss of Kathleen is important to the novel. Almost inevitably, Fitzgerald dramatizes Stahr's misery by showing him drunk. Fitzgerald takes a chance by showing his great man behaving foolishly, for Stahr has no capacity for alcohol. The drunken fight with Brimmer, though inspired by Stahr's unhappiness at the loss of Kathleen, does connect with the executive theme of the novel: Stahr is so accustomed to taking personal responsibility for everything that he even tries to beat up the communist himself.

5 /

The Unwritten Episodes

IT IS POSSIBLE TO MAKE INFORMED GUESSES AT THE MATERIAL TO BE covered in the rest of Fitzgerald's outline-plan by extrapolating from his working notes. However, the notes are undated and cover a period of some two years—with early and late material intermixed. The discussion that follows is based on the last version of Fitzgerald's outline-plan.

On 14 December 1940—a week before his death—Fitzgerald prepared a schedule for writing episodes 17–30 in a month, dividing the work into four 7,000-word units. His projection that the novel could be completed in 28,000 words seems low in view of the amount of action remaining.

> New Schedule from Dec. 14–Jan. 15th inc.
>   (Have done 36,000 words)
> Conception One day
> Plan   " "
> Write four days at 1750 a day
> Notes, letters + rest one day.

This should finish me up at 7000 words a week. (The assumption is that the episodes average 1750—they must be made to do so. In the planning try to divide the work into seven thousand word units, roughly.

The Storm breaks to the Meeting of Four
Wylie White to Lieing low
Last Fling to the Airport
The Plane to the Funeral (short one)

18. The Cummerbund—market—(The theatre with Benchley) August 10th

The only clue to the content of this episode is Sheilah Graham's
recollection that Fitzgerald was intrigued by her story that she had
once rejected a suitor because he was wearing a red cummerbund.[1]
The application of this anecdote to the novel remains a mystery.
Benchley, is, of course, humorist Robert Benchley, who was one of
Fitzgerald's Hollywood friends.

19. The four meet, like Hop and Lefty. Renewal. Palomar

The content of episode 19 is another mystery. Hop and Lefty
have not been identified, but Fitzgerald knew Lefty Flynn, a former
college football star and cowboy actor. "Renewal" probably refers to
a resumption of the affair between Kathleen and Stahr. Palomar is
almost certainly a reference to the Palomar Ballroom in Los Angeles, but what was to occur there is unknown. A possible clue to the
Palomar scene is provided by this note: "*Director*. Well, he was
walking along with his early marriage—trying to walk a little in front
of her. Curious loneliness in the Palomar. The old hurt came back,
heavy and delightful. Benny Goodman and Scottie's drummer, so
handsome, chewing gum in time to the music. Moorish, boorish,
garish lights overhead."

20. Wylie White in Office   August 28th–Sept. 14th.

Episode 20 was to deal with the encounter in which White
rebukes Stahr for blocking the Guild—probably a revision of a similar scene cut from Chapter 2. Things are starting to go wrong at the
studio, and Stahr's unity is being broken up because the writers no
longer trust him. As the novel progressed, Stahr would have become increasingly isolated from both his partners and from his employees. The action of Chapter 6 (episodes 17–20) was to cover
eighteen days.

G21. Sick in Washington. To quit?

[In his outline-plan Fitzgerald used G, H, and I to indicate chapter 7–9. See episodes 25 and 28 below.]

Fitzgerald's notes show that Stahr was to make a trip to Washington where he becomes sick. It was probably to have been a business trip—Stahr is scarcely a tourist—but the purpose of the trip remains unknown. Stahr wants to get the sense of Washington, but is too sick to see anything. (The Washington material connects with the presidential theme in the novel.) At this time Stahr considers quitting the studio.

22. Brady and Stahr—double blackmail.   Quarrel with Wylie.

In episode 22 Brady was to attempt to blackmail Stahr into leaving the studio. The only information that Brady can use against Stahr is his knowledge of Stahr's affair with Kathleen, although it is not clear how Brady has learned about it. Stahr was possibly to retaliate by threatening Brady with information he has that Brady arranged for the murder of the husband of his mistress. Some notes on a case involving a 1917 roadhouse raid outside of Boston in which Fatty Arbuckle and some movie executives were charged with indecent behavior indicate that Fitzgerald may have considered adapting this material as the basis for Stahr's counter-blackmail against Brady. At one time Manny Schwartze was to have been Stahr's source for this information. The quarrel with Wylie White is related in some way to episode 20, and it may be that here is where Fitzgerald intended to use the scene in Stahr's office cut from Chapter 2.

23. Throws over Cecelia who tells her father. Stops making pictures. Story conference—rushes and sets. Lies low after Cut.

Apparently Stahr was to be seeing both Kathleen and Cecelia (assuming that "Renewal" in episode 19 means a renewal of Stahr's affair with Kathleen). When he breaks off with Cecelia here, she "tells her father"; but it is not clear what she tells him. Since there isn't much point for Cecelia to just tell Brady that Stahr has stopped seeing her, Fitzgerald must have planned to have Cecelia tell her father something about Stahr that Brady uses against him—probably information about Stahr and Kathleen.

Then Stahr stops making pictures, probably because of his power struggle with the Brady faction. Here Fitzgerald was going to provide a view of Stahr's day in contrast to episodes 7–11, showing the difference in Stahr when he isn't making movies. This episode was to include the crisis over the studio salary cut. Fitzgerald's notes indicate that Brady was going to persuade the writers and other high-salaried people to accept a cut by promising that the salaries of the secretaries would be maintained—and then Brady would cut all salaries. Stahr, who was opposed to any cuts, is outraged by Brady's treachery.

24. Last Fling with Kathleen. Old stars in heat wave at Encino.

In episode 24 Stahr was to have his final sexual encounter with Kathleen. Sheilah Graham thinks that "old stars in heat wave at Encino" was to be based on a heat wave that she and Fitzgerald experienced when they were living on the Edward Everett Horton estate at Encino. Fitzgerald had projected Chapter 7 (episodes 21–24) at 6,500 words.

H25. Brady gets to Smith. Fleishacker and Cecelia. (S. G. & K)   Sept. 15–30th

Chapter 8 was to begin with episode 25, in which Brady reveals to Smith, Kathleen's husband, that she is having an affair with Stahr. Brady was to persuade Smith to agree to some action against Stahr—possibly an alienation of affection suit. At the same time Cecilia has a rebound affair with Mort Fleishacker, the company lawyer, who differs from Stahr in every possible way. "S. G." refers to Sheilah Graham, and "K" probably stands for Kathleen—meaning that Fitzgerald planned to develop certain parallels between Miss Graham and Kathleen. This time span of Chapter 8 was 15–30 September.

26. Stahr hears plan. Camera man O.K. Stops it—very sick.

In episode 26 Stahr was to learn about the action Brady and Smith are planning to take against him, probably from cameraman

Garcia (Zavras) who feels a great sense of gratitude to Stahr. Although Stahr manages to block Brady's plot, his health is failing.

The outline-plan suggests that Fitzgerald may have simplified his story line. His notes indicate that at one time he considered a double-murder plot: upon learning that Brady has arranged to have him killed, Stahr would retaliate. After setting up the murder of Brady, Stahr flies east to establish an alibi, but experiences a sense of revulsion at the realization that he has in effect become corrupted by Brady. Stahr decides to send a telegram from the first airport calling off Brady's murder; however, the plane crashes before Stahr can act. In the planning stages Fitzgerald considered giving Robinson an important role in the murder plot, perhaps having him act as Brady's agent. There is an indication that Fitzgerald's original plan involved Stahr arranging for Robinson's murder. In an early stage of the story Robinson was to have been in love with Kathleen, but this idea was obviously dropped. When Robinson is introduced in Chapter 2 the reader has the feeling that Robinson is being planted for a purpose that will be developed later, but he does not reappear in the episodes Fitzgerald wrote. Sheilah Graham believes that Fitzgerald had decided to cut Robinson out of the novel in the final rewrite.

If Fitzgerald had in fact dropped the murder material, it was a sound decision. Stahr would inevitably be debased by participation in a murder—even allowing for the fact that he changes his mind. For Stahr to arrange Brady's murder goes counter to the characterization Fitzgerald built up. Nevertheless, it is by no means clear that Fitzgerald had really rejected the murder material, for the outline-plan includes "(The Murderers)" in Chapter 8.

27. Resolve problem. Thalia at airport. Cecelia to college; Thalia at airport. S. G.

Episode 27 completes Chapter 8. Here Stahr (or Fitzgerald) was to "resolve problem," but it is not clear which problem—the problem of Kathleen's husband, the problem at the studio, or both. Since Chapter 8 is labeled "DEFEAT" in the outline-plan, it is apparent that Fitzgerald saw Stahr as losing the struggle for control of the studio. Stahr is flying east, probably to consolidate his position with the stockholders in New York (or to establish an alibi), and

Kathleen sees him off. They meet Cecelia, who is returning to college on another plane. Fitzgerald projected chapter 8 at 7,000 words, making it the longest chapter in the novel.

I28. The plane falls. Foretaste of the future in Flieshacker   Sept 30th–Oct.

Episode 28, which opens the ninth and final chapter, was to describe the death of Stahr in a plane crash and the taking over of the studio by Fleishacker, who represents the financial interests. The outline entry for this episode does not mention Fitzgerald's original idea of having the plane wreckage discovered by children whose attitudes toward life are determined by the possessions they find; and Fitzgerald seems to have been undecided about the plan. If this material had been retained, it probably would have ended the novel. This is Fitzgerald's note for the looting of the plane:

It is important that I began this chapter with a delicate transition because I am not going to describe the Fall of the Plane but simply give a last picture of Stahr as the plane takes off and describe very briefly in the airport the people who are on board. The plane, therefore, has left for New York and when the reader turns to Chapter X,* I must be sure that he isn't confused by the sudden change of scene and situation. Here I can make the best transition by an opening paragraph in which I tell the reader that Cecelia's story ends here and that what is now told was a situation discovered by the writer himself and pieced together from what he learned in a small town in Oklahoma, from a municipal judge. That the incidents occurred one month after the plane fell and plunged Stahr and all its occupants into a white darkness. Tell how the snow hid the wreck and that inspite of searching parties that the plane was considered lost and that will resume the narrative—that a curtain first went up during an early thaw the following March. (I have to go over all the chapters and get the time element to shape up so that Stahr's second trip to New York, the one on which he is killed, takes place when the first snow has fallen on the Rockies. I want this plane to be like that plane that was lost for fully two months before they found the plane and the

---

* The reference to the tenth chapter indicates that this is an early note, written before Fitzgerald decided on a nine-chapter structure.

survivors.) Consider carefully whether if possible by some technical
trick, it might not be advisable to conceal from the reader that the
plane fell until the moment when the children find it. The problem
is that the reader must not turn to Chapter X and be confused, but
on the other hand, the dramatic effect, even if the reader felt lost for a
few minutes, might be more effective if he did not find at the beginning of the chapter that the plane fell. In fact, almost certainly that is
the way to handle it and I must find a method of handling it in that
fashion. There must be an intervening paragraph to begin Chapter X
which will reassure the reader that he is following the same story, but
it can be evasive and confine itself to leading the reader astray thinking that the paragraph is merely to explain that Cecelia is not telling
this next part of the story without telling the reader that the plane ran
into a mountain top and disappeared from human knowledge for several months.

When I have given the reader some sense of the transition and
prepared him for a change in scene and situation, break the narrative
with a space or so and begin the following story. That a group of
children are starting off on a hike. That there is an early spring thaw
in this mountain state. Pick out of the group of children three who
we will call Jim, Frances and Dan. That atmosphere is that particular
atmosphere of Oklahoma when the long winter breaks. The atmosphere must be an all cold climate where the winter breaks very suddenly with almost a violence—the snow seems to part as if very un-
willingly in great convulsive movements like the break-up of an ice
flow. There's a bright sun. The three children get separated from the
teacher or scoutmaster or whoever is in charge of the expedition and
the girl, Frances, comes upon a part of the engine and fly-wheel of a
broken airplane. She has no idea what it is. She is rather puzzled by it
and at the moment is engaged rather in a flirtation with both Jim and
Dan. However, she is an intelligent child of 13 or 14 and while she
doesn't identify it as part of an airplane she knows it is an odd piece of
machinery to be found in the mountains. First she thinks it is the
remains of some particular mining machinery. She calls Dan and
then Jim and they forget whatever small juvenile intrigue they were
embarking on in their discovery of other debris from the fall of the
plane. Their first general instinct is to call the other members of the
party because Jim who is the smartest of the children (both the boys

ages about 15) recognizes that it is a fallen plane—though he doesn't connect it with the plane that disappeared the previous November) when Frances comes upon a purse and an open traveling case which belonged to the Lola Lane actress. It contains the things that to her represent undreamt of luxuries. In it there's a jewel box. It has been unharmed—it has fallen through the branches of a tree. There are flasks of perfume that would never appear in the town where she lives, perhaps a negligee or anything I can think of that an actress might be carrying which was absolutely the last word in film elegance. She is utterly fascinated.

Simultaneously Jim has found Stahr's briefcase. A briefcase is what he has always wanted and Stahr's briefcase is an excellent piece of leather and some other traveling appurtenances of Stahr's. Things that are notably possessions of wealthy men. I have no special ideas at present, but think what a very wealthy, well-equipped man might be liable to have with him on such an expedition and then Dan makes the suggestion of "Why do we have to tell about this? We can all come up here later and there is probably a lot more of this stuff here and there's probably money and everything." These people are dead— they will never need it again, then we can say about the plane or let other people find it. Nobody will know we have been up here."

Dan bears, in some form of speech, a faint resemblance to Bradogue. This must be subtly done and not look too much like a parable or moral lesson, still the impression must be conveyed, but be careful to convey it once and rub it in. If the reader misses it, let it go—don't repeat. Show Frances as malleable and amoral in the situation, but show a definite doubt on Jim's part, even from the first, as to whether this is fair dealing even towards the dead. Close this episode with the children rejoining the party.

Several weeks later the children have now made several trips to the mountain and have rifled the place of everything that is of any value. Dan is especially proud of his find, which includes some rather disreputable possessions of Ronciman. Frances is worried and definitely afraid and tending to side with Jim, who is now in an absolutely wretched mood about the whole affair. He knows that searching parties have been on a neighboring mountain—that the plane has been traced and that with the full flowering of spring the secret will come out and that each trip up, he feels that the danger is more and

more. However, let that be Frances' feeling, because Jim has, by this
time, read the contents of Stahr's briefcase and late at night, taking it
from the woodshed where he has concealed it has gotten an admiration for the man. Naturally, by the time of this episode all three
children are aware of what plane it was and who was in it and whose
possessions they have.

One day also they have found the bodies, though I do not want to
go into this scene in any gruesome manner, of the six or seven victims
still half concealed by the snow. In any case, something in one of
Stahr's letters that Jim reads late at night decides him to go to
Judge——and tell the whole story which he does against the threats
of Dan, who is bigger than he is and could lick him physically. We
leave the children there with the idea that they are in good hands,
that they are not going to be punished, that having made full restoration, and the fact that, after all they could plead in court that they
did not know anything more about the situation than "finder's
keeper's." There will be no punishment of any kind for any of the
three children. Give the impression that Jim is all right—that Frances
is faintly corrupted and may possibly go off in a year or so in search of
adventure and may turn into anything from a gold digger to a prosti-
tute, and that Dan has been completely corrupted and will spend the
rest of his life looking for a chance to get something for nothing.

I cannot be too careful not to rub this in or give it the substance or
feeling of a moral tale. I should very pointedly that that Jim is all right
and end perhaps with Frances and let the readers hope that Frances is
going to be all right and then take that hope away by showing the last
glimpse of Frances with that lingering conviction that luxury is over
the next valley, therefore giving a bitter and acrid finish to the incident to take away any possible sentimental and moral stuff that may
have crept into it. Certainly end the incident with Frances.

29. Outside the studio. S.G.

Episode 29 was to leave the reader with a final view of Kathleen
outside the studio after Stahr's death. Fitzgerald was attracted by the
irony of the fact that, except for the night of the flood, she has never
been inside the studio. Again this view of Kathleen was to be based
on Sheilah Graham.

The epilogue can model itself quite fairly on the last part of Gatsby. We go back to Cecelia as a narrator and have her tell it with the emphasis on herself so that what she reveals about what happened to her father, to the company, to Thalia seems to be revealed as if she was now a little weary of the story, and told all she knew about it and was returning to her own affairs. In it she might discuss whom she married and try to find an equivalent of that nice point in Gatsby where the narrator erases the dirty word that the boy has scrawled in chalk against the doorstep. I think it might be touching if she met Thalia in this episode and was going to take her through the studio and found that she couldn't do it because she was called East so that the reader knows that Thalia won't ever see the studios and I think that I'll leave Thalia's life in the air, her character unimpaired, deepened without quite the pettiness in the end of Gatsby—Thalia all in all being a fuller and richer person than she had been six months before—released from her particular material bondage to Kiki and perhaps with a little hope embarked on some enterprise that seems to promise a future for her or with the idea that she might marry Robinson, the cutter or even a paragraph which implied that now Thalia was more attractive than she had ever been and that there was no doubt that she was going to be all right. To that extent to reassure the reader and not leave a bitter taste in the reader's mouth about Thalia.

And I think I'll do my own method of ending probably on a high note about Stahr but that will solve itself in the writing. And as toward the end I'll tend to go into a certain cadence prose.

30. Johnny Swanson at funeral

An alternate conclusion for the novel was an account of Stahr's funeral, in which Fitzgerald wanted to present one last large Hollywood irony: Johnny Swanson, the has-been cowboy actor noticed by Cecelia in Chapter 2, is mistakenly asked to be a pallbearer; thereafter his career has a miraculous recovery. Even in death Monroe Stahr is a star-maker.

Fitzgerald based the funeral episode on an anecdote about Irving Thalberg's funeral. Harry Carey, a former cowboy star, was one of the pallbearers—a surprising choice since he was not one of Thalberg's close friends. The story went around Hollywood that Harry Carey received the letter intended for writer Carey Wilson, who was one of Thalberg's closest associates. Bob Thomas refutes this story in *Thalberg* (New York: Doubleday, 1969). At any rate, both Harry Carey and Carey Wilson were pallbearers for Thalberg, and Harry Carey's career did subsequently prosper.[2]

6 /

The Book

SHEILAH GRAHAM SENT THE UNFINISHED NOVEL TO MAXWELL PER-
kins on 11 January 1941, shortly after Fitzgerald's death.

I have today sent air mail and registered a copy of Scott's unfinished novel. It is hard to know where to begin in talking about it.
There are masses and masses of notes, which you will probably want
to see as well; but Scott's secretary has all these, and she only has one
copy of them. When and if you want to see them, I will have her
make copies if you think it necessary.

I don't know whether you knew that the hero of Scott's book was
suggested strongly by Irving Thalberg, who died in the summer of
1936. And I am enclosing a copy of a letter which Scott had penciled
with the probable intention of writing it to his wife, Norma Shearer,
when he had completed the novel. We also found a fragment addressed to himself, which is so very sad. I thought you would like to
see it now.

With the book you will find a large sheet of paper on which, right
at the beginning, he wrote down his plan for the book. He had
changed some of it, of course, but not basically. As you see at the bottom, he was writing the book for two people—for Seventeen as sym-
bolized by Scottie, and for Edmund Wilson at forty-five. His idea was
to interest both generations.

I don't know whether Scott had discussed titles with you. At first
for quite a while, he was going to call it STAHR—which is the name

of the book's hero. But about three weeks before he died, he said to me, with a grin—"What do you think of this title?—THE LOVE OF THE LAST TYCOON." My first reaction was "I'm not sure." And he wasn't sure either. But he was going to sit on it, and then submit it to you and see what you thought. In his papers he had written it down as follows:

THE LOVE OF THE LAST TYCOON

A Western

By F. Scott Fitzgerald

The title has grown on me quite a bit. He wanted it to sound like a movie title and completely disguise the tragi-heroic content of the book.

When you have finished reading it and you want to know how it was going to end, I will get together again with his secretary, and we can put together his latest ideas for the rest of the book. I am aching to know what you think of it. As you know, he would not let me read it—until he had polished the first draft. But he read from day to day the words he had written, and it seemed pretty good then; but not nearly as good as I found it when I actually did read it, which I have just done. *Don't forget this was the first draft.*

Here are some odd notes that you might want to know. In the early part of the book he mentions 'Cecelia' as having gone to Smith College. Later he changed it to Bennington, and it was the latter that he wanted.

The time of the book's action was most important to Scott. I don't know whether this appears in his notes, but he wanted it to be as of five years ago. He places the period with the songs of 1934–5 and by the mention of a few people who were alive or prominent at that time. When I asked him why he had put the novel back a little in the past, he said it would have been quite a different story if he had written of Hollywood today—and that with the death of Thalberg, the last of the Princes had departed. There weren't many others, but I think he regarded D. W. Griffith as one.

You will find he mentions the near-future death of 'Stahr' in two places. He was going to eliminate one of the references when he had completed the first draft. He wanted it to be where it would have most shock effect.

In Episode #8, page 5.—he substituted the name 'Brady' for 'Bradogue.' And when I told him that I thought Bradogue was a much better name, suggesting something rather harsh and ruthless, he said that was why he had changed it. As he went on writing the novel, he apparently decided that Bradogue should not be quite the horror he had intended him to be at the beginning.

The longest episode in the book deals with Stahr's Day. He was not altogether satisfied with what he had done on this, and was going to work it over and possibly cut and change it a great deal.

In Episode #8 and #9—there is a repetition of his description of 'Rose Meloney.' He intended cutting it out from Episode #9.

He was far from satisfied with all of Episode #11, and was going to work quite a bit on that too.

In Episode #16—First Part—Page 3, he wanted the word turkey spelt 'tuhkey'—as it is typed.

About 'Schwartze' in the first episode of the book. Scott told me he would either have to cut him out completely or find some way of bringing him into the rest of the book. . . . On page 19 in the first part, where he describes 'Stahr' as being the head of his gang when he was a boy, a similar idea appears in Budd Schulberg's book, which is coming out in a couple of months, and Scott was going to eliminate this.

There may be quite a few errors on the movie production stuff, but he was going to check all this very thoroughly before sending the book to you.

And that is all. Except here's a copy of the plan he had for Stahr's Day.

P.S. I have initialed the few pencil marks I have done on the copy. Everything else is in Scott's handwriting—with the exception of the word 'English' for British. I was his technical adviser on the English stuff and would have told him to make that change.[1]

Perkins consulted with the executor of Fitzgerald's estate, John Biggs, and with Harold Ober about publication. Although Perkins seems to have initially had reservations about the wisdom of salvaging the work-in-progress on *The Last Tycoon,* it was decided that the material should be published in a collection of Fitzgerald's work. Some consideration was given to the plan of having another writer complete the novel. John O'Hara and Budd Schulberg were tentatively approached by Perkins; both declined. At one point Perkins seems to have considered asking Ernest Hemingway, but Zelda Fitzgerald firmly resisted the suggestion—without mentioning Hemingway's name in her letter: "May I suggest that rather than bringing into play another forceful talent of other inspiration it would be felicitous to enlist a pen such as that of Gilbert Seldes, whose poetry depends on concision of idea and aptitude of word rather than on the spiritual or emotional transport of the author." [2] Then Edmund Wilson agreed to edit the work-in-progress without recompense, contributing his editorial fee to the estate for the benefit of Zelda and Scottie. While Wilson was editing the material he was in touch with Sheilah Graham, who shared with him her knowledge of Fitzgerald's plans. Her 6 March 1941 letter about the ending of the novel was supplemented by her visit to Wilson on Cape Cod.

If Scribner's publish the unfinished manuscript, it should be trimmed a little, don't you think? There are some parts—particularly parts in the Producer's Day that Scott was going to cut down. The manuscript is 37,000 words now, of which Scott would have cut about 6 or 7,000 words. As I wrote to Max Perkins, I could perhaps help on this in pointing out just where he had planned the cuts. Or is it better for someone who doesn't know Hollywood at all—someone who would only know what was interesting from an outsider's point of view to do that?

This is how it was going to end:

Brady was out to ruin Stahr in the same way that at one time, and perhaps all the time, L. B. Mayer was out to wrest control of Metro from and/or to ruin Irving Thalberg. Stahr was almost kicked out and decided to remove Brady. He resorted to Brady's own gangster methods—he was going to have him murdered.

On a 'plane flying back to Hollywood Stahr decides not to go through with the murder, which has already been planned and which other people are doing for him—if he did, he would be as bad as the

Brady crowd. So at the next airplane stop he plans a cancellation of orders. I imagine the murder was to take place within a few hours. Before the next stop, however, the 'plane crashes, and Stahr is killed. Which left the murder to go through.

I think the final scene of all was to have been Stahr's funeral. And Scott was going to use an actual incident that happened at Thalberg's funeral. Harry Carey, a well-known actor in the old silents and popular in the early talkies, had been unable to get a job in pictures for several years before Thalberg died. He did not know Thalberg and was surprised to receive an invitation to act as pallbearer at his funeral. It was considered a great honor and only the most important and most intimate of Thalberg's friends (all of them important) were asked to be pallbearers. Harry Carey—slightly dazed, accepted and big-shots at the funeral were amazed when they saw Carey, presuming he had an inside track of some sort with Thalberg, and as a direct result he was deluged with picture offers and has been working ever since. The invitation was a mistake. It was meant for someone else, whom Scott told me about but whose name I have forgotten.

Scott was going to have at the funeral all the Hollywood hypocrites assembled in full force. I had told him of the Marx Brothers sobbing their eyes out on the day Thalberg died—always making sure they were within crying distance of the 'right' people. Scott was going to have Stahr's spirit say, "Trash!"

The English girl was to remain an outsider in Hollywood—I think one of Scott's notes has that she would never get inside a studio (although that is where Stahr first saw her on that idol floating down with the flood). Cecelia, the narrator, is writing her story in a sanitarium for T.B.'s, and this, of course, would be revealed at the end.

At the point where Scott left off things were to go badly for Stahr in business and love. Many things, although in the plan, would have been changed in the same way that he deviated within the structure of the plot on what he had already written and the plan. In the plan he had the American man the English girl married, a technician or something in the studio. But I think he was going to change that— make him more powerful, put him in the position of damaging Stahr.

I am coming to New York again for a week at the beginning of May. Perhaps by that time something will have been decided about the manuscript. If some or all of it is published, Scott's dying won't be quite so awful. He worked hard and desperately and hopefully on the book, and it would be terribly sad if it were lost.[3]

Most of Wilson's correspondence with Perkins is missing from the Scribners Archives at the Princeton University Library; and his letters to Miss Graham have not been located.[4]

Miss Graham and Frances Kroll, Fitzgerald's secretary, both responded to Wilson's summary of the novel's unfinished parts on 11 June 1941.

[Frances Kroll]

I've read and reread your synopsis. I think you've developed a wonderfully clear plot line, considering the mass of notes you had to wade through. However, I do hope you will not consider me audacious if I make a criticism. Believe me, I only venture to do this because STAHR so completely filled those last months. I feel that after reading the book, to plunge into several pages of outline will not carry through to the end any emotional contact with STAHR. Of course, I realize that the purpose of the synopsis is to give the reader an idea of the way the novel might have continued, but I strongly felt the need of a little padding of Stahr even in a synopsis. The story of Hollywood is not as important as is the conception of Stahr, the man.

Although Scott definitely told me he did not want to make Stahr a hero in the conventional sense of the word and did not want to justify Stahr's manner of thinking, he did want to present it thoroughly and show the cause of Stahr's reactions. Stahr truly believed that because he quickly climbed the ladder from office boy to executive that all other people had the same chance for success—that the day of individual success was still flourishing. I believe that is why Scott satirically considered the alternate title for the book "The Last of the Tycoons." Despite Stahr's genius and artistry he did not "come along" politically.

He believed in infinite loyalty—if you gave people a chance they should play along with you no matter what opposition they might have to your tactics. That was why he quarrelled with Wylie White, whom he had repeatedly given a chance despite White's pranks and drunken habits and who turned after the pay cut even though Stahr had not instigated this cut.

I think, too, it should be emphasized how badly Stahr felt about the pay cut. Brady took advantage of Stahr's absence from the studio to call a meeting of the writers. With a tearful speech he told them that he and other executives would take a cut if the writers consented to take one. If they did, it would not be necessary to reduce the salaries of the stenographers and other low salaried employees. The writers agreed to take the cut and Brady about-faced and slashed the stenographers' salary to a new low anyhow. These are tactics which Stahr's sense of fair play would never have allowed.

You mention something about Stahr's change in status as a producer. Unless this is specified in the notes, I don't think this is so. From what I remember of our discussions, Stahr, inherently the artist, was to make one artistic flop—the kind of picture that would not be a movie "box office hit" but one that would be an artistic achievement. It was to be a picture in good taste and perhaps filled with all the ideas Stahr, the artist has always wanted to see realized on the screen, but which Stahr, the Hollywood producer could not very well make because such a film would not be money-making. It was to be a picture he knew from the start would "lose a couple of million" but which he nevertheless makes to satisfy himself despite opposition from other studio financial heads. (This, I believe, was to be the picture followed in the other "day at the studio).

Forgive me for running on like this, but I truly think a few colorful background facts will make STAHR more memorable even though so much of the novel has to peter out in synopsis form.

If my suggestion has no merit, please just forget it, and if you think it might help, I know your expert critical hand will simmer this letter down to a few sentences rightly inserted.

Many thanks for letting me see the synopsis and if I can be of further help do let me know. With very best wishes.

P.S. I believe Kathleen and Cecelia were to have a scene, a rather friendly one, after Stahr's death, although just how or where I do not know. Is it specified anywhere?

About the ending—the airplane sequence was not definitely set as an epilogue, but was as probable as any other. I believe it was in the original outline of the novel submitted to Mr. Perkins. Are you going to use it at all? [5]

[Sheilah Graham]

Max Perkins sent your notes on how the story ends.

Mark #1. What about the name Smith? That's Kathleen's name—isn't it? * And it is also the name of her future husband—W. Bronson Smith. At first, as you know by the notes, Kathleen was to have been a married woman when she met Stahr. Now she is unmarried when they meet, but still called Smith. Is it confusing to have Kathleen have the same surname as the man she is going to marry? Or doesn't it matter? It probably doesn't.

Mark #2. You say, "A wage cut threatened at *Universal.*" This is the name of a studio in Hollywood, and Scott was anxious to avoid the impression of any particular studio as the place of his story. I don't remember his using the word "Universal" in his story. It might be better in your notes to say "Stahr's Studio" or something like that.

Mark #3. Was it clear that Stahr and Brady were trying to *blackmail* each other? I thought the purpose of wire-tapping was for each to get the goods on the other and that Brady would use it to kick Stahr out of the studio. But Stahr would only use his information to retain his command of studio production. Or is that blackmail anyway?

Mark #4. Did Brady decide to bump Stahr off? Is that in the notes? I didn't know that. I thought Scott had just meant that Brady was a killer when he decided that Stahr should consider using Brady's own weapon—murder—to get his way. On the separate page—which I found a few days ago, there is reference to Brady's past "the affair of the girl's husband murdered." This, I imagine, refers to the philandering of Brady with a woman whose husband he had murdered. Does it sound confused and too melodramatic that Brady should decide to murder Stahr, then Stahr decide to murder Brady—unless, of course, you have notes to this effect—and you indicate this on page 171. through Pete Zavras? Stahr, of course, was going to have Brady murdered, until he decided in the plane against using Brady's own despicable methods and was going to stop it but the plane crashes.

Mark #5. I can't quite remember this, but I thought Cecilia went to see her father in his office to try to get a job for that broken-down actress who knew Kathleen—not for Johnny Swanson—or did she try for both?

---

* Kathleen's last name is Moore. Her friend is named Edna Smith.

And finally, Scott did not altogether have that feeling of hopelessness about the movies as an instrument for reflecting American life and ideals. True, Stahr and Thalberg died—Thalberg because of over-working and straining against enormous odds—and Fleishacker is sort of left in control. But I know for a fact that Scott felt that the day would come when another great figure—another Thalberg or Griffith—would succeed in again doing something fine with the movie medium. Scott, himself, wanted to be a movie director because of what he thought could be done.[6]

Perkins' correspondence with John Biggs shows that Wilson's original plan was to publish *The Last Tycoon* with "The Crack-Up" essays and perhaps the Pat Hobby stories. Perkins opposed this plan, feeling that Fitzgerald had done himself a disservice with "The Crack-Up" and that the Hobby stories were far below Fitzgerald's best short fiction.

The title of the volume published by Scribners on 27 October 1941 read: 'THE LAST TYCOON / AN UNFINISHED NOVEL / BY / F. SCOTT FITZGERALD / TOGETHER WITH / *THE GREAT GATSBY* / AND SELECTED STORIES.'

The stories were "May Day," "The Diamond as Big as the Ritz," "The Rich Boy," "Absolution," and "Crazy Sunday." The size of the first printing is unknown, but it was less than 5,000 copies. The book sold steadily but slowly. A second printing was required in 1941; it was reprinted in 1945, 1947, and 1948.

The reviews were good, with many critics taking their lead from Wilson's assertion that *The Last Tycoon* is Fitzgerald's "most mature" work. The statement that it would have been Fitzgerald's masterpiece was not unusual. Stephen Vincent Benét's assessment in *The Saturday Review of Literature* attracted considerable attention: "You can take off your hats now, gentlemen, and I think perhaps you had better. This is not a legend, this is a reputation—and, seen in perspective it may well be one of the most secure reputations of our time." [7]

THE LAST TYCOON IS THE most promising unfinished work in American literature and the one that has received the most serious critical attention. Indeed, the appreciation of this fragment has tended to obscure its fragmentary nature. On 21 December 1940, the day of his death, Fitzgerald had written about half of a *working* draft, for he had completed the 17th episode of a 30-episode outline; however, at this point he had consumed 44,000 words of his 51,000-word projection. Many structural problems remained unsolved. The amount of plot action still to be developed in the unwritten portions—the double blackmail, the Washington trip, the resumption of Stahr's affair with Kathleen, the union struggle, the studio pay cut, the plane crash, the funeral—strongly suggests that Fitzgerald would have needed another 50,000 words to complete his plan.

The only published text of *The Last Tycoon* is still the one Edmund Wilson edited in 1941. At that time he was performing an act of friendship on behalf of a writer who was generally regarded as a failure. Wilson's edition was adequate for its time and purpose: to salvage Fitzgerald's literary remains and bring in a little money for the estate. Now Fitzgerald is a major figure whose final work-in-progress merits careful study. A definitive edition of *The Last Tycoon* is overdue.

The editorial problem for a definitive edition of *The Last Tycoon* involves two concerns: preparing a text of the work that preserves Fitzgerald's intentions, and identifying Wilson's emendations. The second concern is important because the Wilson text is the only text that has been available for thirty-five years; therefore all of the criticism of *The Last Tycoon* has been based on Wilson's emended text, which has shaped the evaluation of the novel.

The editorial situation for *The Last Tycoon* is obviously different from that of novels which their authors saw into print in that we simply don't know what Fitzgerald's final intentions would have been. We can only determine what his intentions were in the latest drafts—which are not final drafts. Fitzgerald's writing habits required layers of revision, but it is a relatively clear-cut matter to establish the sequence of drafts and to identify the latest one.

Even in a work which the author saw through the press we can have little confidence in the accidentals (spelling and punctuation)—which include a quantity of house styling, since normally the author has to accept most of the accidentals imposed on his work in the proofs. But at least we know that the author saw the proofs and had the opportunity to act on any serious distortions of his style. For an unfinished work like *The Last Tycoon* we can only guess at the texture of pointing the author would have sought. The problem is particularly difficult in the case of F. Scott Fitzgerald, who was accustomed to accepting certain kinds of styling—but who also was an inveterate reviser in proof. Indeed, Fitzgerald seems to have regarded proofs as a kind of typescript which afforded him the opportunity to revise and rewrite: *The Great Gatsby* did not achieve its final structure until Fitzgerald reworked it in galleys.

Fitzgerald's punctuation presents a serious editorial problem in *The Last Tycoon*. He never learned the rules of punctuation, and depended on his editors to attend to purely formal matters of punctuation. For example, he did not know how to punctuate dialogue, habitually using commas instead of periods before a new sentence of speech—thus: "It's my busy day, Red," said Stahr tensely, "You lost interest about three days ago." Such matters require emendation and present no difficulty. But Fitzgerald's punctuation within sentences is a difficult problem. He punctuated by ear and had what has been called perfect pitch for the sound or rhythm of a sentence. His manuscripts show that he always punctuated lightly to preserve the flow of his sentences—omitting the commas that other writers would use. Nevertheless, Fitzgerald rarely insisted on his own punctuation. He was amenable to house styling and routinely accepted Maxwell Perkins'—and other editors'—alterations of his pointing. The matter is delicate and far from simple. Although Fitzgerald was an unorthodox punctuator who expected styling, he nevertheless seems to have had a system. Unlike his spelling, which was simply bad, Fitzgerald's punctuation probably does represent his preference. Wilson repunctuated *The Last Tycoon* according to the rules; but a case can be made for preserving Fitzgerald's punctuation when it is not demonstrably wrong or confusing. The principle for editing *The Last Tycoon* in 1977 should be to present a conservatively-emended text that reflects the work-in-progress nature of the material—with all emendations from the copy-text stipulated in apparatus.

Wilson did not deliberately exaggerate the completeness of the manuscript, and he carefully noted in his Foreword that "the text which is given here is a draft made by the author after considerable rewriting; but it is by no means a finished version." Yet Wilson's edition distorts the state of Fitzgerald's progress by treating the material as chapters. For example, Wilson comments that at the time of his death Fitzgerald "had written the first episode of Chapter 6." Fitzgerald's outline for his novel breaks it down into 30 episodes forming 9 chapters (outline episode 17 is the opening of outline Chapter 6); but after Chapter 1 Fitzgerald stopped writing complete chapters. Thereafter the novel exists only in episodes or sections that Wilson assembled into 6 chapters on the basis of the author's outline. This point is worth stressing, for it shows that Fitzgerald was having structural difficulties and intended to shape the chapters in a later revise.

The novel will always be known as *The Last Tycoon*, but a symptomatic problem is that there is no authorial source for this title. The only title page included with the manuscripts reads "Stahr / A Romance." Another title in Fitzgerald's notes is "The Love of the Last Tycoon / A Western"—which Wilson may have modified. Sheilah Graham's memory of the title is not clear, but she thinks she may have told Wilson that "The Last Tycoon" was one of the titles Fitzgerald was considering; however, it is not mentioned in her 11 January 1941 letter to Perkins.[8] Frances Kroll Ring wrote Wilson that "The Last of the Tycoons" was "the alternate title." In any case, Wilson provides no source for *The Last Tycoon* title, and there is no evidence that it was Fitzgerald's final choice.

The key decision for any edition is selection of copy-text—the form of the work which is the basis for the edited text, the text which the editor will emend. For *The Last Tycoon* the selection of the copy-text involves a choice between Fitzgerald's manuscripts and Fitzgerald's revised secretarial typescripts. Given Fitzgerald's habits of composition, the decision is clear: copy-text for *The Last Tycoon* should be the latest revised typescripts. The manuscript drafts are not to be disregarded, however, for they should be checked for whatever evidence they can provide about cruces in the typescript. Although Fitzgerald revised each level of draft, he did not collate them; and some typing errors were not corrected.

There is no problem about Edmund Wilson's selection of copy-text for *The Last Tycoon*. He correctly used the latest corrected

typescripts for his edition. One does not have to be a disciple of Sir
Walter Greg to make obvious decisions about copy-text. Since Wilson was preparing a text for the general reader, he freely emended
Fitzgerald's typescript drafts. Some of his emendations were necessary—such as the regularization of names. *Brady* is named *Bradogue* in the early episodes, but Fitzgerald's notes make it clear that
Brady was his final decision. Pete Zavras, the cameraman, who,
though clearly Greek, is named Pedro Garcia in all drafts. (Only
Fitzgerald could have named a Greek character Pedro Garcia.) In
his notes Fitzgerald reminded himself to change Garcia's name, but
he provided no substitute for it. It seems clear that the name Pete
Zavras was supplied by Wilson. It is a suitable name, but the reader
ought to know its source. At one point Wilson emended a Zavras
speech in a way that can be challenged. In the typescript he says to
Stahr, "You are the Aeschylus and Diocanes of the moving picture.
. . . Also the Esculpias and the Minanorus." Wilson emended the
speech to: "You are the Aeschylus and the Euripides of the moving
picture . . . Also the Aristophanes and the Menander." But Wilson's confidence in his erudition betrayed him. *Diocanes* indicates
that Fitzgerald was trying to write *Diogenes*—not *Euripides*. One
might contend that Fitzgerald was merely listing names from classical civilization for their sound, but the emendation of *Esculpias* to
Aristophanes destroys the point of Zavras' elaborate compliment.
Esculpias was Fitzgerald's spelling for *Aesculapius*, the god of medicine. Since Stahr has determined that there is nothing wrong with
Zavras' eyes, it is proper for Zavras to compare him with Aesculapius. Fitzgerald knew exactly what he was doing in this case. In this
same passage Wilson interpolated the phrase "the Oedipus who
solved the riddle" after Zavras has referred to Stahr as "The Delphic
oracle."

Although Wilson's substantive emendations are not wholesale,
some are clearly unjustified. His edition omits phrases and entire
sentences; for example, this description of the effect of Stahr's voice:
"He was like a brazier out of doors on a cool night." The Wilson
text alters—probably unintentionally—Kathleen's "opalescent
brow—the coco-colored curly hair" to "opalescent brown, the cool-
colored curly hair." Fitzgerald's "closer than an embrace" becomes

"slower than an embrace." None of the emendations in the Wilson text is identifiable by the reader.* However, the emendations in the published form of *The Last Tycoon* are not necessarily all Wilson's. After Wilson corrected and revised Fitzgerald's typescripts, a new typescript was prepared for printer's setting copy. Further departures from Fitzgerald entered the book text in the retyping and proofing stages—and may well be the result of independent emendation or inattention by the Scribners copy-editors. The setting-copy typescript survives, but the proofs do not.

The kind of edition Edmund Wilson delivered in 1941 as a labor of friendship was determined by two factors. First, there was the nature of the job that Scribners expected: a reading text for a popular audience. A definitive edition was not wanted and would not have been published. Indeed, it would have seemed absurd under the circumstances. The second factor was Wilson's confidence—often indistinguishable from arrogance—in his abilities. He felt superior to Fitzgerald, whom he had patronized for more than twenty years. This attitude made Wilson less than the perfect editor for *The Last Tycoon*.

F. Scott Fitzgerald left 17 episodes or sections for a novel that was still evolving: not 5 complete chapters; not two-thirds of a novel. Yet Edmund Wilson's treatment of the manuscript obscures the gestational nature of Fitzgerald's work and misleads readers into judging work-in progress as completed stages. Some of the critics who have protested that *The Last Tycoon* has been overpraised have perhaps reacted from a sense that the published text does not represent Fitzgerald's final decisions. The best way to assess *The Last Tycoon* is to read it as Fitzgerald left it—or in a printed edition that preserves the work-in-progress nature of that form.

What is needed is an edition of *The Last Tycoon* that emulates Samuel Johnson's claim for his edition of Shakespeare: "I have rescued many lines from the violations of temerity and secured many scenes from the inroads of correction."

---

* An editorial apparatus for *The Last Tycoon* has been deposited at the Princeton University Library, the Library of Congress, the British Library, the Caroliniana Library (University of South Carolina), and the Lilly Library (Indiana University).

Appendix

Notes

Acknowledgments

Appendix

Fitzgerald's Notes

THE MATERIAL FOR *The Last Tycoon* INCLUDES MORE THAN TWO hundred pages of notes: character sketches, outlines, plot ideas, bits of dialogue, descriptions, biographical material about Irving Thalberg, background on Hollywood, and two hollywood stories ("Last Kiss" and Director's Special"). Nearly all of this material is in typescript, indicating it was either typed from Fitzgerald's holograph or dictated by Fitzgerald. The pages are not consecutively numbered, and the order of the material probably changes whenever a scholar handles it.

Edmund Wilson granted himself considerable flexibility in preparing a selection from Fitzgerald's notes for publication. In addition to correcting spelling and punctuation, Wilson omitted parts of notes and conflated notes.

Some of the more useful or interesting of Fitzgerald's notes follow. They are printed here exactly as Fitzgerald left them, but an attempt has been made to group them into notes on the novel and general notes. The spacing between entries in the notes has not been preserved.

NOTES ON THE NOVEL

The morale of the studio, Stahr's morale, had survived the expansion, the arrival of sound and, up to this point, the crash and the depression. Other studios had lost identity, changed personel, changed policies, wavered in subjection to Eastern stockholders, or meekly followed the procession. But Stahr's incalculable prestige had created an optimism only equalled by that of the River Rouge plant in its great days.

Some of the conversation in the long day more sexy in tone. Not too much and in good taste.

For Stahr: Call from a red-head (35 yrs. old) His refusal. I think this is necessary if it is not sordid.

Change Garcia to a Greek

Explain his attitude towards authors and how it was like the attitude of Bernard Shaw's attitude in the preface to "Plays pleasant and unpleasant." That is, he liked them, but to some extent he saw them as a necessary evil. How thereafter, he developed the process of having the author working behind another, practically his invention; his ideas about continuity, how the links of the chain should be very closely knit rather than merely linked.

Very funny scene of Aldous Huxley trying to be a regular scenario writer and Sidney Franklin against. Huxley quoting Wells whom he thinks of as a popular writer ("Wells—he's had some success here hasn't he?") Quotes: "Wells says in some early novel we're all Hegelians in spite of ourselves and perhaps the 31st member is a communist and the 4th is double talk man."

Tracing Stahr biologically through a day in terms of blood pressure. Did he take coffee? Was it all will? Did he rest well?

Must describe Thalia *definitely* the first time he really sees her.

La Borwitz. Joe Mank—pictures smell of rotten bananas.

Curiously calm, soft voice as if his words were a sort of poetry.

The idea of a certain great film which Stahr has long planned— a very rough subject or irreligious. An original. And have the censor interfere.

Be sure the solution of the director incident is not too neat. Keep the coat thing but somehow remove the smarty superman element with a little irony.

Firing director seems a small thing to do unless someone else is scared, or director is fierce and brutal.

He was under no illusion about success—the varying components of its make up. For instance he was right a little more often than most men but this was trebly reinforced by his habit of saying things in an utterly assured way, no less forceful for being soft. He knew that the intuitional proportion of superior rightness in his thoughts was simply incalculable importance—he knew also that it might cease at any time but this was something he did not like to think about.

General low autocracy a la Louis XI with observers (le barbier) Acute attention and quick weighing. Quite pleasant without warmth. Knows the value of praise. Distrusts theatrics—hence Nunnaly's success with him.

Stahr tells someone a plot half in Yiddish.

Correction: Ridingwood Scene—
You didn't want to work with Lewin did you King?
I couldn't stand it Monroe.
You didn't want these scenes rewritten.
If I can have my own man. I don't want some writer like X who doesn't know his ass about pictures sit here and kibitz.
Stahr's face flexed. He reached out suddenly and tore open King's blouse the great buttons bursting off to the floor. (one button?)

They never really see the ventriloquist for the doll. Even the intellectuals like to hear about the pretentions and extravagances and vulgarities—tell them pictures have a private and complex grammar like politics and automobile production or society and watch the blank look come into their faces. I could try for instance to make you understand what Stahr meant by his peculiar use of the word "nice" something like what St. Simon meant by La Politesse—and you would classify what I had said as a lecture on taste.

Free from the presentiment that any of his disciples will deny or even contradict him. This was the later trouble.

Kept an amazing amount of detail in his head. Could spend a day *aiding* in the cutting room, *editing* and *photographing* or *working on continuity* of a dozen different pictures besides keeping his office appointments. Was a creative artist, was never pompous, always extremely *considerate* to others. (Sheilah's report)

Stahr subscribes heartily to what the perfume trade might call the law of packaging—that a mediocre scene in a sleek flacon is a better commodity than the perfumes of India in a tin can. MGM pictures are always superlatively well-packaged—both the scenes and personalities which inclose the drama have a high sheen. In general he is betting on good taste as nationally salable.

The situation on the big lot was that every producer, director, and scenarist there could adduce proof that he was a money maker. With the initial distrust of the industry by business, with the weeding out of better men from the needs of speed, with the emphasis as in a mining camp on the lower virtues; then with the growing complication of technique and the exclusiveness it created—it could be fairly said of all and by all of those who remained that they had made money—despite the fact that not a third of the producers or one twentieth of the writers could have earned their living in the East. There was not one of these men, no matter how. low grade and incompetent a fellow who could not claim to have participated largely in success. This made difficulty in dealing with them.

For Guest—Died: Prince Aage of Denmark, 52 veteran officer in the French Foreign Legion; after brief illness; in Taza, French Morocco. Cousin of King George V, Tsar Nicholas II, King ChristianX of Denmark, King Haakon VII of Norway, King Constantine of Greece, he renounced his rights to the Danish throne when he was 26. Said he then: "It wasn't such a sacrifice." Don't divulge who he is until far in the scene.

"One of the Bauberg brothers is waiting in Mr. Brady's office. It's either Jefferson or Moe."
Stahr chuckled.

"It's Jefferson—that was Moe on the phone. This afternoon Charles'll phone and I'll run into Abe tomorrow. The Old brother game—work in shifts and wear you down—"

"I think they want to borrow—"

Above all her beauty was a great mass of dyed hair that looked like nothing else but that. He knew that played a part in what had attracted him. She looked like a whore—he was wearied of "ladies," the middle class actress who became haute bourgeoise or the authentic plutocrats that gravitated toward or around the industry. Half of the girl was like the etc. etc.

A few little unattached sections of her sun-warm hair blew back and trickled against the lobe of the ear closest to him, as if to indicate that she was listening.

The long-haired, set-faced, I-won't-act young actors.

Must solve the forgotten author problem. Perhaps in the studio chapter. Make a joke of him from the producer's angle.

If you think there are a lot of attractive young men around Hollywood you are wrong. There are handsome males but even when their names are Brown or Jones or Robinson they seem like the type you can find on any cheap beach in Italy. Like the oranges and lemons they are plentiful and large but they have no taste. That's why I went with Wylie White. He was a southerner and at his worst he had a code to violate. It was fun to watch him doing it.

This will concern itself with Cecelia's love for Stahr and the episode will concern itself with her discovery of her father.

(a) This episode begins with Cecelia taking up the story directly and describing an affair she was having with a young man. Have her describe it just as women do when they feel that they will be more convincing by telling almost everything and leaving out the main thing rather than the second method which, of course, is wiser for women not to mention anything or any incident about which they are not prepared to reveal the whole truth. That is, she tells our listener, our reader, our recorder a lot about this affair which was engrossing her attention at this time, but always casually reassuring him that while there had been a lot of struggling, she had preserved her "virtue" Have her make a great emphasis on this enough so that perhaps the wisest of the readers may think "she does protest too much." Nevertheless let her in a burst of conventional self-righteousness think that she has convinced the reader that her relations with this undetermined man are essentially not most extreme. Now at this point, either by an accidental meeting on her way to see her father on the lot or perhaps because Stahr has sent for her thinking she could do something for Thalia—something he has planned for Thalia, perhaps something in the nature of a job or some sort of work that Thalia's interested in.

In the scene that takes place, she, Cecelia the narrator, should realize the depth of her love for this man at its fullest and I would like to do some very strong, quiet writing there to describe her feelings. In the writing, Cecelia should appear at her best and at her most profound. It is rather her feeling about Stahr that I want to describe than an objective picture of Stahr at this particular point. I want to find some new method of describing this. Some method in which everything that surrounds him assumes a magical touch, a magical quality without resorting to any of the old dodges of her touching the objects that he touches. I want her feelings to soar to the highest pitch of which she is capable and I want her in this episode to, for the benefit of the reader, to set away everything tawdry or superficial in her nature. This should be one of the strongest episodes in the book.

Now when the episode with Stahr is over, I want her to leave his office and have outside his office, a tremendous reaction from this exaltation and in this reaction I want her to tell the reader or the recorder the truth about the fact that she had given herself to this other man the night before—whom she has no intention of marrying, perhaps an almost experimental gesture.

She turns a man down in narrative, then to readers' surprise: Except that I did sleep with him—that afternoon. I'd rather you'd put that in too.

I went to the screen actors ball. I shall not describe it. Suffice to say the lights shone over fair women and brave, not very brave men.

If the ball room of the Ambassador that night had been the Sistine Chapel Stahr could have covered it with innumerable figures like Michael Angelo.

Scotty comes up to people when she meets them as if she were going to kiss them on the mouth, or walk right thru them, looking them straight in the eye—then stops a bare foot away and says her Hello, in a very disarming understatement of a voice. This approach is her nearest to Zelda's personality. Zelda's was always a vast surprise. (Celia imitates another girl in this)

This girl had a life—it was very seldom he met anyone whose life did not depend in some way on him or hope to depend on him.

Reinforce sense of a deep rich past with Minna—he brusquely says to Kathleen that it can never be the same. Her reaction is in spunkily saying the same, but knowing it's comparatively in a minor key.

Shaken by the flare-up they go back, she still thinking she can withdraw. She could not bear to think. It was tonight. It is a murky rainy dusk, a dreary day (change former time to sunset) They left the hotel a little more than three hours ago but it seemed a long time. Get them there quickly. Odd effect of the place like a set. The mood should be two people—free—He has an overwhelming urge toward the girl who promises to give life back to him—though he has no idea yet of marriage—she is the heart of hope and freshness. *He seduces her because she is slipping away*—she lets herself be seduced because of overwhelming admiration (the phone call). Once settled it is sexual, breathless, immediate. Then gentle and tender for awhile.

Her voice and the drooping of her eyes when she finished speaking like a sort of exercise in control, fascinated him. He had felt that they both tolerated something, that each knew half of some secret about people and life, and that if they rushed toward each other there would be a romantic communion of almost unbelievable intensity. It was this element of promise and possibility that had haunted him for a fortnight and was now dying away. (half used)

Wise and fond and chokingly sweet as it had been with Minna when sometimes they had gone for many days.

Physical attraction not clear. Time lapses wrong. Indicate desire and confidence and have it grow.

Women having only one role, their own charm—all the rest is mimicry.

Kathleen is physically attracted. Also playing with idea that she might marry him right away. But her debt makes her dismiss this.

He is struck again by her beauty which must be redescribed, her manner, her gestures, way of talking, style, content. It becomes apparent to Stahr that she has a great deal of culture—from the Baron-Goldbeck man.

She says something smart and he sees it's in another world and gets her to say it again and again. She fascinates him like some writers. She thinks what a long way she's come. I'd better like it and it starts *may be* a certain jealousy.

The phone in the workman's shed actually rings and she catches a glimpse of his power which he hadn't intended. It fascinates her. He represents action. He hadn't intended to answer the phone.

Meets Bugsy Siegel out on bail in Brady's office.

This is Celia taking up the story. I should probably explain why I spent so much of the summer hanging around the studio. Well, for one thing I was too big to keep out now and I knew how to do it without bothering people. I had had a difference with Wylie White about who had the say about my body so there was ——— ———, whom I didn't intend to marry who was playing the man who *al*most got the girl in three pictures at once and had to be on the lot. And thirdly, most important I had nothing else to do. (Finish with description of Hollywood boys.)

"A man offered to cut somebody's throat for me last week," said Stahr.
"You're just drunk with power."
Stahr was amused. That was the way Wylie White talked to him but no girl had ever talked to him like that before.

It is doubtful if any of these head men read through a single work of the imagination in a year. And Stahr who had no time whatever to read and must depend on synopses began to doubt that any of his supervisors read more than what was ordered; he doubted that his casting people (note for a character here) covered the range he would have wanted them to. A show played a year and a half in San Francisco—the speciality in it was discovered only after it reached Los Angeles where the young teats of a girl show drew a tired satiated audience and the specialty was in a boom market within a week. And had to be paid for against important budgets where alertness would have bought it for nothing.

Stahr as a sort of Rimbeau. Precocity and irony which is born young.

Origin of "fair play" as it began to extend to the bourgeoise. and the proletariat (about 1840 then 1880). It was formerly exclusive to chivalry.
Stahr accepting it with the American tradition. Bradogue not. Bradogue a mere survival morality—slums of Dublin or Manx. Like Sicily.

Stahr had had more men and women that loved him than anyone he knew, but whether that made him a scoundrel or leader he didn't know.

Stahr overhearing a conversation between gentiles about Jews. A sharp cutting scene. The effect on him in toto.
Stahr: Those men won't want to make good pictures after I'm gone—

Stahr didn't die of overwork—he died of a certain number of forces allied against him.

Stahr's memory of Dartmouth where he never went—delirium.

Question of girl using the phrase S——house of the world. Possibly make this half heard. Stahr turns around hardly believing, thinking it's someone else. It haunts him—later makes her pronounce it.

Men who have been endowed with unusual powers for work or analysis or ingredients that go to make big personal successes, seem to forget as soon as they are rich that such abilities are not evenly distributed among the other men of their kind. So when the suggestion of a Union springs out of this act of Baird's Stahr seems to reverse his form, join the other side and almost to ally himself with Baird. Note also in the epilogue that I want to show that Stahr left certain harm behind him just as he left good behind him. That some of his reactionary creations such as the Screen Playwrights existed long after his death just as so much of his valuable creative work survived him.

Stahr wants to see Washington. Goes there and is sick the whole time and sees it only as he leaves.

Bradogue who is great on the horses and has long rebelled against what he thinks of as Stahr's idealism and extravagance in the picture business, seeing cuts made in other industries is taking advantage of a special situation. The situation is that Stahr who is in the East has fallen ill and has succumbed to a complete nervous and physical breakdown affecting his heart so that what he thought would be a four or five day trip devoted largely to discussion with certain blocks of stockholders has become a conference around a sickbed. Stahr who has previously been in general good health, though conscious of a growing fatigue, has the natural rebellion of an active man and of what the doctor says and asks for a specialist. The specialist confirms what the doctor said and gives Stahr what amounts to an ultimatum: That is a death sentence unless he stops here and now and rests himself in some quiet way. He suggests a trip around the world or a year off or anything that will divorce him from work.

The idea fills Stahr with a horror that I must write a big scene to bring off. Such a scene as has never been written. The scene that to Stahr is the equivalent to that of an amorous man being told that he is about to be castrated. In other words, the words of the doctor fill Stahr with a horror that I must be able to convey to the laziest reader—the blow to Stahr and the utter unwillingness to admit that at this point, 35 years old, his body should refuse to serve him and carry on these plans which he has built up like a pyramid of fairy skyscrapers in his imagination.

He has survived the talkies, the depression, carried his company over terrific obstacles and done it all with a growing sense of kingliness—of some essential difference which he could not help feeling between himself and the ordinary run of man and now from the mere accident of one organ of his body refusing to pull its weight, he is incapacitated from continuing. Let him go through every stage of revolt.

Meanwhile, however, the stockholders are meeting around his bed and only by certain things that he lets slip to them does he divulge what is going on inside himself. However, enough has been divulged so that there have been telephone calls to Bradogue and Bradogue himself has gotten in touch with both doctors and in his winning way, posing as Stahr's friend, found out the truth that Stahr is definitely an unwell man. All this Cecelia finds out from her father on her return. Once again, we see Cecelia at her best, not as a very effectual character, but again as a person who under certain circumstances might have been quite a person. She tells the recorder or the reader how she got in touch with Rogers and was rather surprised to find that Rogers had been re-hired before Stahr left (she has heard, of course, about how Stahr found him in his office, in fact she has heard everything that is told in the book). Rogers knows that the whole lot is in a ferment and that various meetings are being called.

We are going to cut at this point to the meeting of camera men (cutters) at which Robinson will be present.

Episode C.

This meeting will be very briefly summarized—these men being only medium salaried and as a rule not very thoughtful men or very articulate men and are very easily bamboozled into taking this 50% cut that Bradogue is going to put over in Stahr's absence. At the end of the meeting, Robinson should be summoned from the meeting or called aside in almost a mysterious way suggesting to the reader that there is some significance in his being called away though this is a fact that will not be explained at this time. We will go from here to what I hope will be a big scene in which Bradogue asks the directors, writers, supervisors to accept a 50% cut which he says he is going to accept himself, using as his argument, to their surprise and rather to their confusion, the specious argument that by accepting this they will save those in the lower salary brackets—the secretaries from $12. a week up and the prop boys, etc., to whom the drastic cut would mean a terrible hardship. He gets over his idea for two reasons— one because the amorphous unions—though the name is not used—which are called into being among workers with common interest such as directors and writers are split by jealousies and factual disagreements, certain of them for example, have never even thought of themselves as workers and some are haunted by the old fashioned dream of communism and Bradogue is wise enough to use every stop on the organ including personal ties to increase these differences and to rule by dividing. In any case, he wins his point to the great disgust of those of the writers who are the more politically advanced or the shrewdest and who detect in this a very definite manifestation of a class war reaching Hollywood.

Episode D.

We will go from here, by the very quickest way, to an office where Cecelia is talking to a secretary who happens to be a personal friend who has helped her as a reader and who was called to the office of the chief of secretaries and now we learn that the whole thing has been a frame-up—that a great proportion of the secretaries are going to be laid-off without warning, that extensive cuts are to be made in their pay of 40% instead of 50% but still the very things that he has made his point by promising to avoid, are going to happen. Women with families to support are going to find that they have scarcely enough with which to buy bread and that they are without jobs and no chance to get a job in any other studio for to a certain extent, other studios have waited for this studio to start cutting and then take the same steps.

When Stahr is sick he keeps saying give it back to the directors again. Don't leave it with these men. Give it back. I took it away from etc. (Rearrange)

The blind luck that had attended the industry, and he knew the croupiers who raked in the earnings of that vast gambling house. And he knew that the Europeans were impressed with it as they were impressed with thesky-scrapers, as something without human rhythm or movement. He was tired of his own rhythm and the rhythms of the people in Hollywood. He wanted to see people with more secrets than the necessity of concealing a proclivity for morphine.

Stahr had a working of technics but because he had been head man for so long and so many apprentices had grown up during his sway more knowledge was attributed to him than he possessed. He accepted this as the easiest way and was an adept though cautious bluffer. In the dubbing room, which was for sound what the cutting room was for sight he worked by ear alone and was often lost amid the chorus of ever newer terms and slang (get this up). So on the stages. He watched the new processes of faking animated backgrounds. Moving pictures taken against the background of other moving pictures, with a secret child's approval. He could have understood easily enough often he preferred not to preserve a sensual acceptance when he saw the scene unfold in the rushes. There were smart young men about—Rienmund was one—who phrased their remarks toconvey the impression that they understood everything about pictures. Not Stahr. When he interfered it was always from his own point of view not from theirs. Thus his function was different from Griffith in the early days who had been all things to every finished frame of film.

Baird and Stahr go into terrible row about pay-cut and at the same time all his writer friends desert him on the Film Guild issue.

What would I be as Stahr's wife—another Mrs. Rich Bitch of Beverly Hills. I could promote him from Beverly Hills to Pasadena except he wouldn't want to be promoted.

I'll pay for passion—so will the public. But it's rare, and it doesn't consist of being born on Grand Street, and sometimes it wears out.

Incident of Stahr calmly telling off an agent he was an overgrown errand boy. Implication, you can get away with it with writers who are soft but not with him. Something like quarrel of Knopf with Swanie.

There is a place for a hint somewhere of a big agent to complete the picture. Myron or Berg though—no mercy for Swanson.

In order to forgive Stahr for what he did that afternoon it should be remembered that he came out of the old Hollywood that was

rough and tough and where the wildest bluffs hold. He had manu-
factured gloss and polish and contour of new Hollywood but oc-
casionally he liked to tear it apart just to see if it was there.

It's fun to stretch and see the blue heavens spreading once more,
spreading azure thighs for adventure.

Dash Hammet's exit for Wylie—good plot.

Stahr is miserable and embittered toward the end.

Never wanted his name on pictures—"I don't want my name on
the screen because credit is something that should be given to others. If you are in a position to give credit to yourself then you do not
need it."

Suddenly outdated he dies. (accidentally, naturally, murdered)

And they build the Stahr Building.

Harry Cary gets Cary Wilson's invite. A new career

A brilliant producer, Stahr, has everything, but has lost his wife
whom he loved. He meets her image, falls for her, finding in mid-
channel that he is breaking up a good marriage.

He leaves her, takes up with another girl, and is plunged into a
growing row in his business which gets worse and finally strikes him
down in Washington. On his return his ambitious partner has done
some dirty tricks. Stahr calls him and in his disgust throws over the
man's daughter, returns to the girl and tries for a divorce.

His enemy strikes by going to the jealous husband. Stahr takes
counter-measures then seeing it makes him as low as what he is
fighting he gives up and goes away—with no future that he sees.
The plane falls.

Brady and Stahr are ostensibly great friends but Brady wants him
out—Schwartze tries to warn him. Stahr meets the English wife of a
cutter and is haunted by her. He meets her half secretly at the football—everywhere except at his office. There is absolutely no privacy
and the seduction finally takes place at Malibu in his unfinished
house.

Cecelia knows all this and it breaks her heart. But nobody
knows, including her, who the girl really is. She inadvertently tells

her father who discovers who the girl is and immediately sees his chance—he goes to Stahr, threatening him in a pleasant way and suggesting he marry Cecelia but Stahr counters with what he knows about Brady (the affair of the *girl's husband murdered*—Stahr has found it out from his wife's trained nurse when he died.)

Stahr's problem is whether to quit or go on in the face of inevitable discovery. He and Kathleen are taking breathless chances. Now the storm breaks and everyone he had counted on turns against him. He plays with the idea of marrying Cecelia as the best way of getting out and is seen everywhere with her. The reds see him as a conservative—Wall Street as a red. He has one last fling with Kathleen, tells Cecelia about it—throws her over and goes to Washington where he falls sick, with worry.

Meanwhile Brady gets the news to the cutter who has long suspected something. Robinson (who is ———) feels it's the perfect anti-semitic smear gets backing and prepares the bomb.

Knowing nothing of this Stahr gets word of the salary cuts and comes west sick. Kathleen gets word to him. He goes to work and crushes the whole thing by doing just what Brady did—plan to have *Robinson killed*. The clock has gone around. He leaves Hollywood *for an alibi*—in the air he decides against it. The plane falls.

Kathleen is ruined. She never went inside a studio.

Brady killed Stahr. The Academy dream. *Artists get more than bosses.* The phone companies trying to milk them. Collective bargaining. How Warner protracted salary cuts. "You trying to tell me how to run my business." Collecting from him. His revenge— wrecking the Academy. Stahr not making pictures at the end—only going through the motions. Lying low—his own company. He was in Europe when the banks were closed and the committee met agreeing to the cuts. Mayer's company did not need the cut. Smaller companies would have gone broke. He used to faint all the time toward the end. His political opinions (?) Grousing about taxes. His selfishness.

For Mankiewicz—the ten days that shook down the world.

These blows hit Stahr all at once. But at first he has them in control. It is not till they hit his great picture which should be planted back in 10., that he realizes what they mean. He should quarrel with the writers in such a way as to effect the great pictures.

Paradox about Stahr the artist standing for reaction and corruption and ——, and the people who stood for all the good things were horrible.

For Schwartze

A midnight frolic of four years ago at Mishawum Manor, a roadhouse in Woburn said to be conducted by a woman known as Brownie Kennedy, whose guests included several motion picture producers was described today at the hearing on a petition for the removal of Nathan A. Tufts, District Attorney of Middlesex. Attorney General Weston Allen preferred charges that Tufts was concerned in a conspiracy by which the *motion picture men paid $100,000 to escape prosecution* threatened on account of their presence at this dinner party.

The affair took place on March 6, 1917. It followed a dinner to *Fatty Arbuckle* at the Copley Plaza. 20 or 25 people were at this party and there were 10 or 12 women at the house. The company remained from midnight until 4 a.m. *The bill was $1050.* Abrams who was president of the New England Baseball League said he paid it.

The affair was referred to as "drunken affair." There was a conference at Tufts' office. Coakly, Boston Attorney, said if he could prove the men were innocent he hoped Tufts would drop it. District Attorney said that if complainents could be gotten off his back he would not prosecute them. *Lasky, Zukor,* Walter Green, Abe Berman were present at the "drunken affair." It was agreed that all the complainants would be satisfied and the *lawyers fees for $100,000* would be paid. They wanted to have time to prove the men were innocent. Tufts agreed to grant the time.

Two checks of $85,000 were investigated. They were said to be paid in full settlement of *a case growing out of this incident.* There were releases signed which were submitted to Zukor and Lasky and Abrams who denied recognition of the signatures on the releases.

There was no trace that Tufts got any of the $100,000 to hush up this affair and it was finally settled.

How Brady got his start?

The day Stahr died everyone on the lot (including the Marx Brothers) were crying and trying to see who was watching them. "Trash," I could hear him say. "Trash."

A scene where a communist insults Stahr *intolerably*, belittles his whole life.

The Love of the Last Tycoon
A Western
by
F. Scott Fitzgerald

Remember my summing up in Crazy Sunday—don't give the impression that these are bad people.

These are the picture people. Do not blame them too much. I am sure you would do much better in their place if you had all that money to spend and that strange story of what happened to—to produce. We all have one story. But what would you do after that and that and that day after day after dozens hundreds thousands and ten thousands of time.

He did not love anyone at all because the dead did not count. It was not fair to love the dead.

Her Father bought her a Christian but she didn't like it.

Stahr with my theory of what success is: learning from precursors and inferiors and then cutting them to pieces even though they are better men.

P. 174—Chateaubriand—"There are men," said he to Metternich, "who believe themselves universally competent because they have one quality or one talent. Among such men is Chateaubriand, who goes in for opposition because I will not employ him. The man is a reasoner in the void, but he has great powers of dialectic. If only he would use his powers within the lines laid down for him, he might be useful, but he will do no such thing, and so is no use at all. A man must either know how to govern himself or submit to orders. He can do neither the one nor the other, so he must not be given employment. A score of times he has offered himself to me, but rather as though to bend me to his imagination—which always leads him astray—than to obey me. I have refused his services; that is to say, I have refused to serve him."—Does it apply to Stahr?

Don't make her Tarkington.

Cecelia does not tell the story though I write it as if she does whenever I can get the effect of looking out.

Let the glamor show as from far away. Cling to reality, for any departure from a high pitch of reality at which the Jews live leads to farce in which the Christians live. Hollywood is a Jewish holiday, a gentiles tragedy. Stahr should be half Jewish like Hunt. Or is this a compromise. I think it is.

Schwartz typifies the excitement of going to this mining town the same way that some unidentified people might typify a lot of miners approaching gold settled in Alaska. It is necessary that this episode shall have that and also a definitely sexual touch again without compromising Cecelia in the reader's eyes.

The man who has struggled madly for a pot of gold and had his finger tips on it and it has slipped away and now he has gone a little bit crazy in his attempts to catch up with it and that very intensity (typified by his trying to meet this man who is in the private compartment and who will later develop as Stahr) is making a pot of gold more and more inaccessible to him.

Important that he knew the business side first. His submission of a scenario was probably a very quaking venture on his part—very timorous. He must have had no more aesthetic education after finishing secondary school than I did. He had to pick the whole thing up out of the air not even by reading though probably he did some—still in all he probably learned pictures from pictures and naturally got his sense of realities from acute observation and men. He was therefore as unliterate a man as you can imagine in regard to formative influence.

Plant his anonymity—his many plans. Your contributions can't be measured. They have to pay in statue. On his deathbed that haunts him. Maybe a statue.

I must not alienate the reader from her at the beginning, but must give the feeling that "well, I don't like this girl much, but I am going to stick around and see what she has to say because she has let drop a few things that make me think that given the right circumstances she might have been worthwhile."

Nevertheless, the first episode must close with something definitely arresting or shocking about herself.

Action is character.

Consider transferring strong scenes to rear.

He had to leave school *on account of illness* and took a job at his grandfather's dept. store, where he *taught himself to type* in his spare time. He then felt ready for bigger things and put an ad in the paper for a job. "Situation wanted—secretary, stenographer, Spanish, English. Highschool education. Inexperienced. $15." He got four answers and took a job in an importing company.

While he was on the make Stahr was as shrewd, ruthless, and opportunistic as the next man, but he arrived quickly after only a short breathless struggle, and once arrived he found it easier to be fair and generous and honorable than not to be. So he granted the premises on which he was founded—he was a better man than most of us, less bruised, less fearful, and less corrupt.

The girl must be humble; there is a lack of humility in Wolfe, Saroyan, Schlessinger that I find as depressing as O'Hara's glooms.

I want to tell also of his great failing of surrounding himself with men who were very far below him—men of the type of Al Lewin and Sam Marx. However, this may have been because of a surety of his health that he felt in his 20's that he himself was able to keep a direct eye on everything and therefore, would have been hindered rather than helped by men who were positive-minded supervisors. His relation with directors, his importance in that he brought interference with their work to a minimum and while he made enemies—(and this is important) up to his arrival the director had been King Pin* in pictures since Griffith made the Birth of a Nation.

Now, therefore, some of the directors resented the fact that he reduced their position from one of complete king to being simply one element in a combine. His interest in the lot itself is important, his utter democracy, his popularity with the rank and file of the studio.

However this is not really thinking out Stahr from the beginning. I must go back into his childhood and remember that remark of his mother "We always knew that Milton would be all right." Perhaps before I get to this chapter, I could have a talk with Sam Marx and find out a little more about his prototype's early life than I know now. What the original circumstances of his parents were, but the best thing to find somebody who knew him as a boy. Remember also that he was a fighter even though he was a small man—certainly not more than 5′6 ½″, weighing very little (which is one reason he always liked to see people sitting down) and Remember when the man tried to get fresh with his wife at Venice how he lost his temper and got into a fight. I gather he must have been a scrapper from early boyhood, probably a neighborhood scrapper. Remember also How popular he was with men from the beginning in a free and easy way, that is to say, as a man that liked to sit around with his feet up and smoke and "be one of the boys." He was essentially more of a man's man than a ladies' man.

There was never anything priggish or self-superiority in his casual conversation that make men uneasy in the company of other men. He used to run sometimes with a rather fast crowd of directors—many of them heavy drinkers though he wasn't one himself. And they accepted him as one of themselves in a "hail fellow, well met spirit" that is: in spite of the growing austerity which over-work forced on him in later years, Stahr never had any touch of the prig or the siss about him and I think this was real and not an overlay. To that extent he was Napoleonic and actually liked combat—which leads me back to the supposition that probably he was a scrapper as a boy and had always been that way. If, after he came into full power, he sometimes resorted to subterfuge to have his way that was the result of his position rather than anything in his nature. I think, by nature, he was very direct, frank, challenging. Try to analyze what his probably boyhood was from the above.

This chapter must not develop into merely a piece of character analysis. Each statement that I make about him must contain at the end of every few hundred words some pointed anecdote or story to keep it alive. I do not want it to have the ring of an analysis. I want it to have as much drama throughout as the story of old Laemele himself on the telephone.

I would like this episode to give a picture of the work of a cutter, camera man or second unit director in the making of such a thing as *Winter Carnival* accenting the speed with which Robinson works, his reactions, why he is what he is instead of being the very high-salaried man which his technical abilities entitle him to be. I might as well use some of the Dartmouth atmosphere, snow, etc. being careful not to impinge at all on any material that Walter Wanger may be using in *Winter Carnival* or that I may have ever suggested as material to him.

I could begin the chapter through Cecelia's eyes who is a guest at the Carnival, skip quickly to Robinson and have them perhaps meet at a telegraph desk where she sees him sending a wire to Thalia. But by this time and through the material I choose—photographing backgrounds for the snow picture—I should not only develop the character of Robinson as he is, but leave a loophole showing the possibility of his being later corrupted. In a very short transition or montage, I bring the whole party West on the Chief, Cecelia perhaps with friends of her own coax the producer who has been in charge (ineffectual producer) and Robinson.

A plant is necessary at the beginning of this chapter to show that for a period of several weeks Stahr and Thalia had been parted—perhaps two weeks would be enough (also for the mechanics of this chapter, it is necessary that it shall happen at least six weeks after the first affair of Stahr and Thalia in order that his house may be complete and furniture installed and the place in good running order).

The break between Stahr and Thalia has been of Stahr's making. I may or may not show the scene in which this occurs, but Stahr's motive is roughly:

"I am not going to marry this girl. My plans do not include marrying again. She hasn't the particular shine, glamor, poise, cultural background that would make her the fitting match for this high a destiny toward which I seem to be going or this position in which I find myself; therefore, I am really indulging myself by cutting her off from Robinson who is obviously a fine fellow, who adores her and would be a good provider and a good husband." The break has affected them in different ways though this doesn't emerge until later in the chapter. It has given Stahr a great restlessness which is more than merely physical because the girl has bitten into him rather deeply emotionally; Thalia, being more of a realist and more inclined as women are, to accept the inevitable. It has begotten an impatience and restlessness which leads to Thalia's break with the ex-wife or widow, Katherine. The break comes in such a way that she finds herself in an almost desperate position and now she makes the realization that many American women must have made during the depression that she has absolutely no "skill." That there is no position, however humble, to which she is really qualified—she couldn't even make up a bed in a hospital in the proper way. In a rather frightening two or three days, she discovers this.

She considers some course of training such as a secretarial school, but finds that she hasn't adequate funds for this and that it takes more time than she imagined. Perhaps she knows how to peck at a typewriter. She considers wildly this plan or that and on a very hot, dreary afternoon in Los Angeles when she has come about to the end of her resources (—forgot to say that she now has broken entirely with Robinson and is too proud to call upon him) Perhaps a scene if it is not too hackneyed in which she is offered a job with the concealed suggestion that she would have to be nice to some man to hold it—though if I use this, it must be done in some absolutely new way because it is a somewhat hackneyed situation;—she has taken on that day a room in a boarding house, which room happens to be unfurnished, but the landlady is going to supply furniture during the day.

She reaches home at an extremely low pitch thinking of fairly desperate measures—there is something about coming back to the room and finding nothing in it except a chair and a picture upon the wall upon which the landlady seems to place great value (the bed and rugs and other things are to arrive later) which makes more vivid her state of utter desolation.

And at this point, Stahr comes in. She stands up and they come together in a second, clinging together in a great wave of emotion.

On her part composed of love, relief, gratitude, complete losing herself in him—on his part, a full realization of how much he has missed her, of the terrific appeal that she has for him physically and psychologically and spiritually. For a while they just cling together and then he almost, literally, picks her up and takes her out of the house, paying the landlady and takes her, puts her in his automobile and they ride together to his house in Malibu.

At first, for some hours, *they share an overwhelming joy.* They eat together and make love, cling together at times, each cannot bear to let the other out of his sight. The reunion has been so strong in its emotional implications that it seems to the reader as well as to Stahr and Thalia that it is the prelude to an immediate marriage and almost a fade out and a happy ending. At some point though, during that same evening or perhaps the next morning which would be necessarily then a Sunday, something happens (invent some detail or small instant) which gives Stahr the idea: *After all, this is not what I intended. I didn't intend to marry this girl. It is against the logic of my life.* The premises that I set out for myself when I was young do not include this. The cold part of Stahr has crept in a little, not the cold emotion, but the cold part of his mind and almost at the instant in which he realizes and *shows it perhaps by some flicker of his expression,* Thalia who by now is as close to him as if she had lived with him for fifty years, knows it and makes up her mind what to do.

Stahr goes to his office thinking, "well, that can be decided later" and find it the beginning of the situation which will later take us with Stahr to New York and will later culminate in the doings of Chapter 9. When he comes back that night, he finds Thalia gone and a note from her telling him that it's better that they don't enter into any such alliance and the note is written in a way that will touch the reader, but because of these absorptions Stahr for once, doesn't realize its full import, especially as almost immediately necessity arises for him to leave for New York.

STAHR
A Romance
by
F. SCOTT FITZGERALD

GENERAL NOTES

In thirty-four and thirty-five the party line crept into everything except the Sears Roebuck Catalogue.

It is the custom now to look back ourselves on the boom days with a disapproval that approaches horror. But it had its virtues, that old boom: Life was a great deal larger and gayer for most people, and the stampede to the spartan virtues in times of war and famine shouldn't make us too dizzy to remember its hilarious glory. There were so many good things. These eyes have been hallowed by watching a man order champagne for his two thousand guests, by listening while a woman ordered a whole staircase from the greatest sculptor in the world, by seeing a man tear up a good check for eight hundred thousand dollars.

Fastest typist isn't best secretary. Swinburne. Trick golfer with watch, lightening calculator, kicker, et. Faulkner and Wolfe are those.

Sid Perleman is effete—new style. He has the manners of Gerald Murphy and almost always an exquisite tact in prose that borders on the precieuse. I feel that he and I (as with John O'Hara and the football-glamor-confession complex) have some early un-disclosed experience in common so that at this point in our lives we find each other peculiarly sympathetic. We do not need to talk.

Sheilah noted his strange grace doing his interpretation of "Slythy" in the Charade the other night.

I like his brother-in-law West. I wonder if he's long-winded as a defense mechanism. I think that when I am that's why. I don't want to be liked or to teach or to interest. That is my way of saying "Don't like me—I want to go back into my dream."

I know Nat through his books which are morbid as hell, doomed to the underworld of literature. But literature. He reminds me of someone. That heaviness. But in the other person it could be got used to—in Nat it has no flashes except what I see in his eyes, in his foolish passion for that tough and stupid child Mc——. Sid knows what I know so well that it would be blasphemy to put it in conver-sation.

Nine girls out of ten can stand good looks without going to pieces though only one boy out of ten ever comes out from under them.

There are no second acts in American lives.

That moment I felt from time to time with Zelda that she has unravelled the whole skien—that I am speaking with the lightly rolled skien before me, not wanting to disturb it. That even in my most alone and savage and atavistic moment I am doing so. Note Rousseau went a little crazy after finishing the Contract Sociale.

I wasn't precocious, I was merely impatient (or hurried?)

As a novelist I reach out to the end of all man's variance, all man's villainy—as a man I do not go that far. I cannot claim honor—but even the knights of the Holy Grail were only striving for it, as I remember.

Native Son—A well written penny dreadful with the apparent moral that it is good thing for the cause when a feeble minded negro runs amuck.

Biography is the falsest of the arts. That is because there were no Keatzians before Keats, no Lincolnians before Lincoln.

As soon as a man is made a producer he gets to be two things—a son-of-a-bitch and Bernard Shaw.

A FABLE FOR TED PARAMORE *
⟨(Then whom there is no one to whom it is less necessary)⟩
by
F. Scott Fitzgerald

A great city set in a valley, desired a cathedral. They sent for an eminent architect who designed one distinguished by a great central tower. No sooner was it begun, however, than critics arose who objected to the tower calling it useless, ornamental, illogical, and what not—destroyed his plan and commissioning another architect to build a cathedral of great blocks and masses. It was very beautiful and Grecian in its purity but no one ever loved the cathedral of that

---

* Fitzgerald's collaborator on the screenplay for *Three Comrades*.

city as they did those of Rome and Sienna and the great Duomo of Florence.

After thirty years wondering why, the citizens dug up the plans of the first architect (since grown famous) and built from it. From the first Mass the cathedral seized the imagination of the multitude and fools said it was because the tower pointed heavenward, etc., but one young realist decided to dig up the artist, now an old man, and ask him why.

The artist was too old to remember, he said—and he added "I doubt if I ever knew. But I knew I was right."

"How did you know if you don't know your reasons?"

"Because I felt good that day," answered the architect, "and if I feel good I have a reason for what I do even if I don't know the reason." So the realist went away unanswered.

On that same day a young boy going to Mass with his mother quickened his step as he crossed the cathedral square.

"Oh I like our new cathedral so much better than the old," he said.

"But the academy thinks it's not nearly so beautiful."

"But it's because of the mountains," said the little boy. "Before we had the tower I could see the mountains and they made everything seem little when you went inside the Church. Now you can't see the mountains so God inside is more important."

That was what the architect had envisioned without thinking when he accidentally raised his forfinger against the sky fifty years before.

There's no such thing as a "minor" character in Dostoevski.

The episodic book (Dos P. and Romaine, etc.) may be wonderful but the fact remains that it is episodic, and such definition implies a limitation. You are with the character until the author gets tired of him—then you leave him for a while. In the true novel, you have to stay with the character all the time, and you acquire a sort of second wind about him, a depth of realization.

The purpose of a fiction story is to create passionate curiosity and then to gratify it unexpectedly, orgasmically. Isn't that what we expect from all contacts?

Tender is less interesting toward the climax because of the absence of conversation. The eye flies for it and skips essential stuff for they don't want their characters resolved in desiccation and analysis but like me in action that results from the previous. All the more reason for *emotional* planning.

The great homosexual theses—that all great pansies were pansies.

Ernest Hemingway and Ernest Lubitsch—Dotty "We're all shits."

I talk with the authority of failure—Ernest with the authority of success. We could never sit across the table again.

People like Ernest and me were very sensitive once and saw so much that it agonized us to give pain. People like Ernest and me love to make people very happy, caring desperately about their happiness. And then people like Ernest and me had reactions and punished people for being stupid, etc., etc. People like Ernest and me———

As to Ernest as a boy—reckless, adventurous, etc. Yet it is undeniable that the dark was peopled for him. His bravery and acquired characteristics.

Ideas on Fear as being removed as well as profit motive. We know the latter can—but the former. Some day when the psycho-an are forgotten E. H. will be read for his great studies into fear.

Nevertheless value of Ernest's feeling about the pure heart when writing—in other words the comparatively pure heart, the "house in order."

An inferiority complex comes simply from not feeling you're doing the best you can—Ernest's "drink" was simply a form of this.

It is so to speak Ernest's 'Tale of Two Cities' though the comparison isn't apt.* I mean it is a thoroughly superficial book which has all the profundity of Rebecca.

* *For Whom the Bell Tolls.*

I want to write scenes that are frightening and inimitable. I don't want to be as intelligible to my contemporaries as Ernest who as Gertrude Stein said, is bound for the Museums. I am sure I am far enough ahead to have some small immortality if I can keep well.

I am the last of the novelists for a long time now.

Notes

Chapter 1: PRELIMINARIES

1. Frank MacShane, *The Life of Raymond Chandler* (New York: Dutton, 1976), p. 150.

2. See Michael Millgate, *American Social Fiction* (Edinburgh & London: Oliver & Boyd, 1964). Millgate notes that Lord Charnwood's *Biography of Abraham Lincoln* quotes contemporary references to Lincoln as "The Tycoon" (p. 124). Charnwood's biography was one of the books that Fitzgerald assigned to Sheilah Graham in the "College of One."

3. *F. Scott Fitzgerald: The Last Laocoön* (New York: Oxford University Press, 1967), p. 3.

Chapter 2: BACKGROUNDS

1. Fitzgerald Papers, Princeton. The mis-spelling of Thalberg's name resulted from the fact that this letter was dictated. Neither Miriam Hopkins nor Fredric March was under contract to MGM at this time.

2. *Mayer and Thalberg: The Make-Believe Saints* (New York: Random House, 1975), pp. 222–23.

3. John Kuehl and Jackson Bryer, *Dear Scott/Dear Max* (New York: Scribners, 1971), p. 223.

4. *Thalberg* (New York: Doubleday, 1969), pp. 267–68.

5. Marx to Bruccoli, 26 October 1975.

6. *Last Tycoon* notes, Fitzgerald Papers, Princeton.

7. *Last Tycoon* notes, Fitzgerald Papers, Princeton.

8. Fitzgerald scrapbook, Princeton; reproduced in Scottie Fitzgerald Smith, Bruccoli, and Joan P. Kerr, *The Romantic Egoists* (New York: Scribners, 1974), p. 184.

9. *The Real F. Scott Fitzgerald* (New York: Grosset & Dunlap, 1976), p. 174.

10. Bruccoli and Jennifer Atkinson, *As Ever, Scott Fitz—* (New York & Philadelphia: Lippincott, 1972), p. 250.

11. Andrew Turnbull, *The Letters of F. Scott Fitzgerald* (New York: Scribners, 1963), pp. 16–17. Hereafter notes as *Letters*.

12. Sheilah Graham has recounted her life with Fitzgerald in *Beloved Infidel* (New York: Holt, Rinehart & Winston, 1958), *College of One* (New York: Viking, 1967), and *The Real F. Scott Fitzgerald*.

13. See *The Four Seasons of Success* (New York: Doubleday, 1972) and the introduction to the re-issue of *The Disenchanted* (New York: Viking, 1975).

14. *The Four Seasons of Success*, p. 134.

15. Schulberg to Bruccoli, 19 March 1976.

Chapter 3: PREPARATION AND COMPOSITION

1. An excellent study of possible connections between these two projects is Kermit W. Moyer's "F. Scott Fitzgerald's Two Unfinished Novels: The Count and the Tycoon in Spenglerian Perspective," *Contemporary Literature*, XV (Spring 1974), 238–56. Professor Moyer argues that both works should be read in light of the impression *The Decline of the West* made on Fitzgerald, and that Kathleen's explanation that she was being educated to read Spengler is a clue to the meaning of the novel.

2. *Dear Scott/Dear Max*, pp. 253–54.

3. *Dear Scott/Dear Max*, p. 256.

4. *As Ever, Scott Fitz—*, pp. 388–90.

5. New York Public Library.

6. *Letters*, pp. 61–62.

7. *Last Tycoon* notes, Fitzgerald Papers, Princeton.

8. Fitzgerald Papers, Princeton.

9. Scribners Archives, Princeton.

10. 19 October 1939, New York Public Library.

11. *Dear Scott/Dear Max*, p. 258.

12. Fitzgerald Papers, Princeton.

13. Wire, 31 October 1939, New York Public Library.

14. Fitzgerald Papers, Princeton.

15. New York Public Library.

16. New York Public Library.

17. Scribners Archives, Princeton.

18. Joseph Bryan, III to Bruccoli, 9 September 1975. There is a 1 December 1939 wire from the *Post* to Fitzgerald in the Fitzgerald Papers at Princeton: "FIRST INSTALLMENT RECEIVED FROM SCRIBNERS BUT SECOND HAS NOT ARRIVED. EXPECT MONDAY. WILL COMMUNICATE IMMEDIATELY AFTER READING="

19. Fitzgerald Papers, Princeton.

20. Scribners Archives, Princeton.

21. A carbon copy of Fitzgerald's letter of apology is with the Fitzgerald Papers at Princeton.

22. Scribners Archives, Princeton.

23. "Dearly   Beloved"   was   posthumously   published   in   the

Fitzgerald/Hemingway Annual 1969 and collected in *Bits of Paradise* (New York: Scribners, 1974).

24. On 20 May 1940 Fitzgerald supplied the $2300 figure to Perkins; but Sheilah Graham reports in *The Real F. Scott Fitzgerald* that he received $1000 for rights to the story plus $400 a week for ten weeks. The duration of Fitzgerald's work on the "Babylon Revisited" screenplay—which was also called "Honoria" or "Cosmopolitan"—is not clear; there are scripts dated August 1940. It appears that he worked on it intermittently during the spring and summer.

25. Frances Kroll Ring to Bruccoli, 22 April 1975.

26. O'Hara's account of reading Fitzgerald's working draft is in "Certain Aspects," *The New Republic*, CIV (3 March 1941), 311.

27. Fitzgerald Papers, Princeton.

28. *Letters*, p. 349.

Chapter 4: THE DRAFTS

1. For an analysis of Fitzgerald's writing methods, see Bruccoli, *The Composition of Tender Is the Night* (Pittsburgh: University of Pittsburgh Press, 1963) and *The Great Gatsby: A Facsimile of the Manuscript* (Washington: Bruccoli Clark/Microcard Editions Books, 1974).

2. "I have just remembered why Scott had changed the name of BRA-DOGUE to BRADY. He disliked the first as the name for Cecilia—he wanted something less harsh for the teller of the story."—Sheilah Graham to Mary McCarthy Wilson, n.d. (c. June 1941). Princeton.

3. Gabrielle Winkel's "Fitzgerald's Agge of Denmark," *Fitzgerald/Hemingway Annual 1975*, pp. 131–32 suggests that the source for this character was the Swedish count Sigrard Bernadotte, an assistant director in Hollywood during Fitzgerald's time there. However, Fitzgerald's note on an obituary for Prince Aage of Denmark (see Appendix) makes it clear that his source was the Dane. Prince Aage, like Fitzgerald's Agge, had served in the Foreign Legion. He published three books about his experiences: *A Royal Adventurer in the Foreign Legion* (1927), *My Life in the Foreign*

Legion (1928), and *Fire by Day and Flame by Night* (1937). Prince Aage died in March 1940.

4. Schulberg to Bruccoli, 11 September 1975.

Chapter 5: THE UNWRITTEN EPISODES

1. *The Real F. Scott Fitzgerald*, p. 183.

2. *Thalberg*, p. 321.

Chapter 6: THE BOOK

1. Scribners Archives, Princeton.

2. Scribners Archives, Princeton.

3. Yale University Library.

4. Henry Dan Piper footnotes an 11 June 1941 Graham-Wilson letter about *The Last Tycoon* in his *F. Scott Fitzgerald: A Critical Portrait* (1965), but it is actually the letter from Frances Kroll to Wilson printed in this study.

5. Yale University Library.

6. Yale University Library. Sheilah Graham's 22 May 1941 letter to Edmund Wilson, answering queries about the novel, is also at Yale.

7. XXIV (6 December 1941), 10.

8. Sheilah Graham to Bruccoli, 15 August 1975: "*THE LAST TYCOON* title. It was a temporary title but he might have used it for the final. Or *STAHR* or *THE LOVE OF THE LAST TYCOON: A Western*. He really wasn't sure. It's my belief that *THE LAST TYCOON* would be the title—It has the same sort of rhythm as *THE GREAT GATSBY*. *THE L.T.* was *SCOTT'S, NOT EDMUND WILSON'S.*"

Acknowledgments

I COULD NOT HAVE WRITTEN THIS STUDY WITHOUT HELP. MY greatest debt is to Scottie Fitzgerald Smith. After that I am indebted to Alexander Clark, Curator of Manuscripts at the Princeton University Library and to his superb staff. Sheilah Graham, Budd Schulberg, Frances Kroll Ring, and Samuel Marx patiently answered question after question. Claudia Drum and her colleagues in the Interlibrary Loan Department of the University of South Carolina Library were marvels of patience and competence.

Some of the travel for this project was made possible by grants from the American Philosophical Society and the University of South Carolina Department of English; and I am particularly grateful to Professor William Nolte, Head of the Department, for making research funds available at two key points.

I am also obliged to Joseph Bryan III, Margaret Duggan, Muriel Hamilton, Burroughs Mitchell, Charles Scribner III, R. L. Samsell, Jeanne Bennett, the microfilm staff at the New York Public Library, Frances Ponick, Peter Shepherd, and Cara White.

I am indebted to the admirable people at the Southern Illinois University Press. The organization of this study owes much to the advice of Vernon Sternberg, Director of the Press.

I greatly benefited from the readings of my Arlyn.

Once again I am grateful to be at the University of South Carolina, where I can get my work done.